T0114013

GOD'S MIMIC

THE BIOGRAPHY OF HAZEL PAGE

By

Carol Ferguson

Order this book online at www.trafford.com
or email orders@trafford.com

Most Trafford titles are also available at major online book retailers.

Print information available on the last page.

ISBN: 978-1-4120-4428-8 (sc)
ISBN: 978-1-4122-3056-8 (e)

Because of the dynamic nature of the Internet, any web addresses or
links contained in this book may have changed since publication and
may no longer be valid. The views expressed in this work are solely those
of the author and do not necessarily reflect the views of the publisher,
and the publisher hereby disclaims any responsibility for them.

*Trafford rev. 08/31/2018*

 www.trafford.com

North America & international
toll-free: 1 888 232 4444 (USA & Canada)
fax: 812 355 4082

# TABLE OF CONTENTS

Chapter                                             Page

3

## ACKNOWLEDGEMENTS

My first words of thanks must be to our Lord and Saviour, Jesus Christ, who calls, equips and finishes. Thank you also, to all the people who encouraged the writing of this book, some with the simple words, "You need to write a book," and some with more tangible help.

A great big thank you to those who did the editing and proofreading: Eva Hudgin, Loretta Bodie, Myrna Forge, Louise Holland, Pauline Boytim, and Hazel Page.

Thank you to all our friends at Central Baptist in Victoria, the Holland Family, Grace Eno, Hazel's sister, Vi, and others too numerous to mention, for your encouragement, love and prayer support.

Thank you to my family for encouraging and believing in me and to those I work with, for their listening ears, and for praying me through computer glitches!

Lastly, thank you, Hazel, for keeping every prayer letter you wrote during your missionary career, for your meticulous attention to detail and your dedication to what God called you to do. Thank you for baring your heart and making every detail available for the telling.

Carol Ferguson
October, 2004

# PROLOGUE

Hazel watched intently as the man ahead of her boldly crossed a log spanning the rugged ravine. Not only did he tread confidently on the narrow log bridge, but he also carried half of her possessions. Tentatively, Hazel put one foot on the log. Her tennis shoes had a tread, but a slip could result in serious injury. Then, with a prayer on her lips, trying not to look at the drop below, she took a step. Arms out, balancing precariously, one hesitant, shaky step following another, she slowly crossed the chasm. The Lord had not asked her to train as a tightrope artist, but that's what she felt like. One final quick step brought her to solid ground. Every part of her being quivered.

Three times in the past three years Hazel Page had been invited by the village people of Langkaan to come to their mountainous region of the Philippines to teach them about the Lord. Three times the people met the requirement to build a house for the missionary and a house for the Lord. Now, after their fourth plea, the mission superintendent had given his blessing. Hazel was on her way.

Two village men, Tiboy and Gabino, guided her over the trail and carried her belongings. This was a one-day trip from Kaagutayan for the local men, but Hazel knew she would slow them down as they made their way across ravines and climbed over boulders as big as a house. Toeholds in the rocks, worn over the years by tribal people, were for bare toes, not for a white person's shoes. It was also that time of the year when people in the Philippines cut down the forest in preparation for their upland rice fields. The trail lay in shambles.

Hazel paused. Using a blade-shaped bamboo stick, she painstakingly scraped several leeches off her legs and dropped them one by one into the bottle of alcohol she carried. Always one for details, she was curious to see how many leeches she would pull off on this trip.

Slowly the trio trudged its way across the rough terrain, one man leading this tall white woman and one following. They neared the meandering Alag River, and now the huge boulders sported blankets of damp, slippery moss. Hazel skidded. Tiboy grabbed her arm, barely preventing a fall to the riverbed below. Shaken, Hazel sat down to remove her shoes. Those few minutes allowed her heart to slow down and her muscles to relax before she continued on, barefoot.

They moved further into the interior. The sky darkened. Torrents of rain poured down and the swift river began to swell. After ten hours of travelling, her dress dripping, her feet burning, Hazel all but collapsed when they stopped for the night. She had not been on a trail that hard for weeks. Even if it meant spending a wet, chilly night in a cave, Hazel was thrilled to be on her way to teach the villagers of Langkaan about the Lord.

By morning the rain had stopped, and when they forded the river it was not so turbulent, although it was still waist deep. Hazel gladly allowed the men to hold her raised arms tightly, so the swift waters would not sweep her off her feet. After the third river crossing, the trail began to climb.

"This is steeper than a ladder up to a rooftop," Hazel thought, as she grasped at roots and rocks to pull herself up. She could tell that her endurance surprised the men. They encouraged her as they continued to clamber still higher.

Finally the group came to a halt. Ahead of them, bark houses sat scattered haphazardly in a little clearing, as if holding back the encroaching vegetation. This was Langkaan. In spite of aching muscles and extreme weariness, Hazel smiled as Gabino pointed to yet another hill. Three new buildings perched like sentinels on the hillside: Tiboy's house, a house for her, and one for the Lord. Hazel's heart swelled with excitement as she thought of the significance of these buildings. The church stood empty, waiting for a congregation. These people trusted her, not only to teach them how to read in a very short time, but also to tell them about the Lord.

Most of the people were still away working. Those she did see held back, as was their custom, allowing time for her body odors to dissipate. Hazel approached the one-roomed house on stilts so lovingly made for her, and in spite of her weariness, scurried up a log ramp, the equivalent of front steps. She had work to do before the people returned from their fields.

The bark walls at each end of her house were only three feet high and even at the peak Hazel could not quite stand up straight. Soon all her belongings lay safely inside, along with several packs of medicine and school supplies she had sent on ahead. She arranged these boxes and her can of water at one end of the room, leaving space near the two-foot-wide door for visitors. The bamboo-slat floor bounced slightly as she worked. Several times her foot almost slipped between the slats.

While Tiboy and Gabino built a shelf for her dishes, she draped her mosquito net above her bed, an oblong piece of bark. The hungry hoards would not be snacking on her!

Then people returned from their fields, and a steady procession of excited, chattering visitors came to welcome her with gifts. White skin and wispy brown hair were a novelty in their village. The fact that a white person was going to live right there with them, if only for eight days, was amazing. Their brown, weathered faces crinkled with smiles as they rushed to help her settle. Cucumbers, sweet potatoes, squash, greens and sugar cane were mounded up under the shelf. Finally darkness, quietness and sleep claimed her, only to be interrupted by the nightly rain and a leaky roof. Hazel pulled a shower curtain from her supplies to cover her bed and slipped into sleep again. The next morning the men quickly repaired the bark shingles. Hazel was ready to go to work.

7

Young and old gathered each morning in the chapel; they filled the benches that lined the walls. Hazel had translated and reduced their Iraya language to writing over the past years, and now she taught them songs, Scripture verses and Bible stories. Excited voices sang out the songs even before they knew the melody. In the back of Hazel's mind was always the question, "Do they really want to know about the Lord or just learn to read their own language?" They stopped briefly for a meal, usually a stew of mushrooms, squash, greens and sweet potatoes. Then the adults went to the fields, and the young people stayed the rest of the day to learn to read.

As she taught, Hazel prayed fervently for each student. A few had previously studied a bit of Tagalog, a similar language, with another teacher, so by the end of the eight days five young people could read. One of the boys bought a Tagalog Bible from her, and as she left the village, Hazel could hear the boy reading aloud from the Gospel of John. Oh, how she prayed that the Word of God would bring forth fruit in the lives of these people!

On the return trip to the lowlands, Gabino again carried some of her supplies. Tiboy remained in the village, and Ben, another villager, took his place as guide, setting a fast pace over a new trail that he had cut. Several times Hazel called for him to wait, but eventually he pulled out of sight. She quickened her pace on the downgrade, searching for a glimpse of him. Suddenly, she slipped, and, still clinging to her two walking sticks, plummeted down the steep incline to the right of the path. Crashing over rocks, branches whipping about her head, she tumbled over and over. With a jolt she landed on a tree trunk the size of an arm; her stomach, the only boneless part of her body, took the impact.

Draped over the tree, Hazel stared down upon a huge boulder and the turbulent river below. In extreme pain she hung motionless, afraid to move lest the tree break. Had she broken any bones? Would she be able to continue the journey? Hazel was reluctant to move and find out, but in spite of her injuries she did thank God for breaking her fall.

Terrified, Gabino slid his way down to where she hung, and rolled her off the tree. "Does this hurt?" He asked in consternation, as he kneaded her abdomen.

"Yes!" Hazel gasped. "That hurts!" Every breath was agony. She hurt all over. As Gabino helped her struggle up to the path again, Hazel noted several good-sized rocks, obviously responsible for the pain in her rib cage.

"So sorry! So sorry!" Gabino apologized and pleaded with her not to blame them.

"God spared my life," Hazel reassured him. "God put that tree there to protect me from the huge rock below and the river."

Bruised and battered, ribs throbbing, Hazel was unable to lift her feet more than six inches. Every step was excruciating. By sitting down and manually lifting her legs, she managed to haul herself over logs that sometimes blocked the way. All along the torturous journey she quoted and sang Isaiah 40:31, "They that wait upon the Lord shall renew their strength, they shall mount up with wings as eagles; they shall run, and not be weary; and they shall walk, and not faint." She kept walking, and the two men watched her.

When they finally stopped to cook some food, Hazel gratefully eased down to the ground. Her shower curtain sheltered the fire from a heavy rain now falling. After eating, Ben insisted that they press on. They followed a logging trail, but Ben's destination was a real road where they could flag down a vehicle and get help for Hazel. Dusk descended and then darkness. The rain stopped and a full moon appeared from behind the clouds, making it possible to see the trail faintly, so they trudged on. When clouds covered the moon, Hazel's little penlight was a valuable asset. Several times Hazel accidentally stepped into ruts, and then she was slogging in agony through knee-deep water. Suddenly they heard barking ahead. Someone had guard dogs running loose, and it would be dangerous to continue on in the dark.

Reluctantly, Ben called a halt to their trek. Hazel was exhausted.

The men again suspended the shower curtain between four poles, and gathered branches and coconut fronds so Hazel would have a dry spot to sit. They were amazed at this feisty white woman. She was in obvious pain, and blood ran down her legs where the wet clothing had rubbed her legs raw. Steam billowed from their clothing as they sat around the fire talking in hushed tones, even yet wary of the dogs.

"How can you be so free from complaining?" The men asked.

"The Lord gives me strength to go on," Hazel replied in Iraya. "He still has a plan for my life. He has work for me to do, teaching people to read His Word and telling them about His love and salvation." The men listened intently as she talked to them. She explained how much she had to be thankful for. She had no broken bones. She could still walk.

"I wish I knew God the way you do," Gabino stated longingly.

"You can know Him in the same way," Hazel told him, her heart offering up a prayer that the men would remember what she had taught them in the past eight days. "Ask Jesus to forgive your sins. Give Him your life and He will be your Lord and Saviour. He will enable you to live for Him." That night, under a full moon, Gabino and Ben prayed and became part of the family of God.

This was only one of the many adventures Hazel Page encountered in her journey to bring the Good News of the Gospel to Mexico, China and the Philippines. This was the reason God laid upon her heart, as a five-year-old, to be a missionary to China. This was why the Lord gifted Hazel, as a three-year-old, to mimic everything she heard.

# CHAPTER 1

## A MIMIC IS BORN

Thump! Crack! "What was that noise?" Hazel's mother wondered at that eerie crack from the living room. Three-year-old Hazel and her brother Irvine were wrestling and bouncing on the soft cushions of the couch.

"Oh, Mommy, my belly do hurt!" That cry of anguish brought her mother rushing from the kitchen. Hazel was on the floor, doubled over in pain. Something serious had happened, but what? After a quick phone call to the doctor, Hazel's father hitched the horse to the covered sleigh, and the young family raced to nearby Unity, Saskatchewan. Hazel's appendix had burst, filling her abdomen with poison. The youngster was writhing in pain, fighting and biting with supernatural strength at anything that came near.

The doctor had to operate immediately. It was the only way to save this beautiful little three-year-old. Perhaps even surgery was too late. Knotting a man's handkerchief, he put it in her mouth to bite on. Seven men held her, so the doctor could administer chloroform. He removed the ruptured appendix and inserted tubes to drain the vile-smelling poison.

"Mommy, the angels are coming for me," the little girl cried out later as she lay in bed, drifting between life and death. Her parents, already much in prayer, prayed even more fervently. "Lord, if you have a plan for Hazel's life, please spare her." Within moments Hazel cried out,

"Mommy, the angels have gone away to heaven again." From that moment she began to improve.

Hazel Annie Page (Annie after her Grandma Page) was born February 11, 1917, in Laura, Saskatchewan. She weighed eleven pounds and was a lazy, contented baby, so chubby that it looked as if cords were tied around her ankles, knees, wrists and waist. In no hurry to move out into the world, Hazel was eighteen months old before she began walking. Up until this time she crawled or skidded along on her bottom, but once she was on her feet she never stopped.

Their rural home was a wonderful place for children to grow up. There were trees to climb and vast open fields in which to run. By the time Hazel was two years old, her sisters Violet and Florence were already attending the nearby one-room school. Brother Irvine, two years older than Hazel, was her playmate, but her brother John, two years younger, would become her soul mate.

Hazel, Florence, Vi, Johnny, Irvine
playing with a rooster.

Hazel grew up a tomboy, but she had an insatiable appetite for learning. She loved to listen to her sisters do their homework in the evening, and no one realized how much knowledge this little girl was absorbing. When Irvine started school, Hazel lost her playmate. Johnny was too young to play the games Hazel invented, so she begged to be allowed to go to school, too. Miss Riddle, the teacher, a frequent visitor in the Page home, agreed to let Hazel come to school as long as she didn't disrupt the classes. Hazel would agree to anything, as long as she didn't have to stay home. So at age four-and-a-half, Hazel began attending school. This was even better than listening as her sisters studied. In the classroom she could listen to all the grades. Like a sponge she soaked up everything she heard and learned to read and write along with Irvine.

Hazel's grandparents on both sides were a vital part of her young life. Hazel and Johnny secretly talked about Grandma Page's *bay window*, referring to her size, emphasized by gathered skirts. Grandpa Page worked in the harness shop. He was good-natured and enjoyed the children's antics. One morning after spending the night at their grandparents' home, Hazel and Johnny emptied all of Grandpa's mouse traps before anyone was awake and hung the mice by their tails on the front gate. When this didn't faze Grandpa, they decided to put a mouse in each of his slippers. Grandpa's bellows delighted them.

Grandpa Hutton always had a bag of warm, freshly roasted peanuts to share with the children and a pocket full of peppermints. He loved to tickle the grandchildren with his soft, bushy beard, causing squeals of delight from his frosty, cold, wet whiskers in the winter.

The family moved to Saskatoon, Saskatchewan, when Hazel was five years old. Mother took the four children to see Mr. Henderson, the principal of the Mayfair School. Violet, Florence and Irvine were quickly assigned to classes. "But you'll have to wait until you're six to start school," he told five-year-old Hazel. What? She couldn't go to school anymore? Broken-hearted, Hazel burst into tears. She sobbed. This wasn't fair! She had learned just as much as the first graders and she cried even harder. Mr. Henderson was amazed to see the child so upset about not attending school. Would it hurt to give it a try? "We'll put her in grade one and see how she gets along." The tears quickly stopped. Within days the teacher complained. It wasn't fair to the other students. Hazel answered all the questions. She was moved into the second grade, and there she stayed.

"Mrs. Page, it has come to our attention that your three youngest children have never been christened," the pastor kindly mentioned after the family had been in Saskatoon for a while. Mrs. Page did not offer an explanation. No one in the family would dare reveal the reason for this "oversight", even though they did snicker about it. Years earlier, when Johnny was tiny, Mother had arranged for the three children to be baptized. The day before the event, Mr. Page came home with his head shaved. His wife refused to go to the front of the church with him looking like that, "not being able to tell which end was up," as she put it, and she cancelled the christening. Now she quickly took steps to remedy the situation. She did not like to be found wanting in any area, so at the Presbyterian Church at Avenue D and 34th Street in Saskatoon, the three Page children were baptized. All was well between family and church again.

It was also in that church that Hazel made a lifetime commitment. A missionary from the China Inland Mission (CIM) was visiting. Hazel sat captivated as the missionary showed *lantern slides* of the Lord's work in China. Imprinted on her heart were pictures of little Chinese children, so adorable and loveable, who had never heard about Jesus.

"I want to go to China when I grow up, to tell the boys and girls and men and women about Jesus," Hazel informed her mother. Mother expected Hazel, like most children, to change her mind many times before she became an adult. But from that day on, when asked what she wanted to be when she grew up, her answer was always, "a missionary to China." She never wavered from that desire.

One day Hazel and Johnny, eyes glowing, sat side by side in the front room, dressed in their Sunday best. If they behaved, they could join their mother for tea when she had visitors. Today a lovely Scottish lady was there for tea. Surprisingly, having tea with Mother's guests was the one occasion when these two active children enjoyed sitting still. Today, the heavy Scottish brogue, the rolled R's and the strange vowels intrigued the children. Listening intently, they silently repeated all she said.

It was an interesting way to spend the afternoon, but soon they could hardly wait for the lady to leave. As Mother went to the door and out onto the front porch to say good-bye to her visitor, the two youngsters looked at each other with twinkling eyes and half-suppressed grins. Without any prompting they began chattering to each other in the exact Scottish accent they had just heard, giggling at each other's attempts. The house grew strangely quiet. Hazel began to try to silence Johnny and restrain herself from laughing. The laughter died suddenly when their mother returned with her eyes blazing. The two women had heard every word.

"I am so embarrassed that my children would mock a visitor to our home," she scolded. "I don't ever want to hear you do that again." The children solemnly promised, but it would be a promise Hazel wouldn't keep. God had implanted in Hazel the unique ability to hear and mimic sounds, an ability to be used in His kingdom.

Hazel and Johnny made a dishwashing crew of two. As soon as supper was over, two dishpans were set up in the pantry, and they went to work. But doing dishes was not a chore for these inventive children. With cue cards hung on the wall, they memorized Bible verses, learned the Shorter Catechism and sang hymns and school songs. Both children had keen minds, and the pantry became a wonderful classroom for the pair. It was also a place where Hazel learned both physical and spiritual facts. One day a soup dish slipped from Hazel's hands. Looking at the broken shards littering the floor, she burst into tears. The family would be hard-pressed to replace even one broken dish. Sorry to have broken it, she also feared getting a spanking.

Florence counselled her little sister to be honest and beg forgiveness when their mother returned from shopping. Then they knelt beside the broken dish and prayed that God would help their mother understand it was an accident and not give her a spanking. Hazel wrapped the pieces in newspaper and waited as the clock ticked off every agonizing second. God answered their prayers. Mother forgave Hazel with a hug and a kiss and Hazel had seen an illustration of how God loves and forgives sinners and answers prayer.

Hazel did get her share of spankings, though, usually for willful disobedience. Her father's milk-delivery job didn't bring in enough to give his five children more than necessities. As the third girl in the family, Hazel's wore hand-me-downs. Her clothes were nice, but other girls in her class had new clothes now and then. When her mother knitted a warm toque for Hazel to wear to school, she detested it. None of the other girls wore toques. Mother was insistent. Hazel had to wear it! Grumbling, she left for school with the cap grudgingly pulled over her light brown hair. When she was almost at the school, she stuffed it into her school bag. At noon, Hazel waited until her friends were out of sight, pulled the toque on and arrived home, secure in her deception. One glance at her mother's face, and Hazel remembered that her entire two-block walk to school through vacant lots was visible from the back window. Her mother had seen the exact moment the toque came off. Hazel had no choice but to confess her disobedience, and take her punishment. With the spanking came an explanation of what she had done wrong. Hazel was surprised later to find that her classmates actually liked her toque.

Hazel loved to visit cousins Stanley, Wyburn, Madeline and Elsie on their farm. Sometimes they would hitch a horse to the buggy, but Hazel preferred riding a horse and was quite proficient at it. One day they were on horseback when a sudden storm blew up. Thunder rumbled and lightning flashed, sending Hazel's horse into a panic.

Hazel sawed on the reins, bracing herself with all her weight, but no matter what she did, that horse was going home. Hazel stayed on as the horse galloped out of control. Suddenly straight ahead she saw the barn. The open door was not high enough for her to stay mounted but the Lord had a plan for her life and wasn't about to let her go. Moments before being slammed face first into the door casing, Hazel slid down the horse's side. She tumbled to the ground shaken but unhurt.

Her mother was not well for most of Hazel's young years. By the time she was eleven, Violet and Florence were out working to help the family financially, and Hazel took over her sisters' chores at home. At night she would set the yeast for making bread and in the morning mix the dough before going to school. At recess she could run the two blocks home to punch the dough down. At noon it was put into eight loaf pans (as many as the oven could hold). They were put into the oven before she returned to school, to be taken out of the oven during her afternoon recess. It was also her job to make sandwiches for her sisters to take for lunch. One day, while making a peanut butter and jelly sandwich for Florence, Hazel licked the oozing jelly off the side of the bread as she always did. But this was not her sandwich. Florence was horrified. Hazel received a severe scolding from her sister and never again licked even her fingers.

Another experience that would follow her throughout her life happened when she was thirteen years old. Hazel was sent to buy a pair of new shoes. The clerk let her choose the ones she wanted and even showed her under an x-ray machine that there was a good deal of space for her foot to grow. On her father's salary, shoes could not be replaced until they wore out, so Hazel chose wisely. These shoes should last a long time, and they did. But no one took into account the speed at which Hazel was growing. Before the shoes wore out, Hazel's big toes were permanently bent up out of shape and would stay that way the rest of her life.

Hazel's intelligence was also growing at an incredible speed. After grade seven, Principal Henderson was pleased to announce that for the first time since he became principal, someone in Miss Wilson's class made 100% on the final English Grammar test—not a single error. "It is Hazel Page." Latin and French were two of Hazel's favourite subjects. She excelled in them, and she and Irvine always conversed in French when they were alone. They were forbidden to speak in French if their mother or anyone else who couldn't understand French was around. Hazel so excelled in French that one day her French teacher took her aside and asked if she would like to go to Paris and train to be a French teacher. The teacher offered to make all the arrangements and also to sponsor Hazel for the time it would take her to finish the course. Hazel was excited and thrilled that she would even be considered for such an opportunity. Paris! Then Hazel politely explained that she had already promised God that she would go to China as a missionary.

Irvine, Mother, Hazel, Vi
Father, Florence, Johnny

# CHAPTER 2

## SORROW AND SALVATION

Hazel's fingers traced the outline of coins inside the envelope. Who would know if she took just one coin? Carefully, without tearing the envelope, she managed to slip a coin out. It was Sunday. Her mother was sick and had entrusted her offering envelope to Hazel. Now aged ten, Hazel was still wearing hand-me-downs, and the peer pressure was building. Sometimes her friends bought candy at recess at the nearby grocery to share with her. She had just found a way to return their friendship. The next day Hazel proudly bought candy to share with those who had given her treats. The second time she took a coin from the offering envelope the guilt was not as acute. She repeated the offence several times. She had found an easy way to obtain money.

As the years passed, Hazel went faithfully to Sunday school and church. In fact, she and her two friends from other churches attended each of the girls' churches every Sunday. Early Sunday mornings they went to the Anglican Sunday school. Later in the morning they attended the Presbyterian Church for both Sunday school and the morning service. In the afternoon they went downtown to the Baptist Church for their Sunday school. In the summer months on Sunday evenings, they went to the Gospel Hall, too. "I knew many Bible verses by heart and had learned the way of salvation," Hazel says, "but I had not made a real commitment to the Lord."

Eventually, Hazel began stealing from Florence's coin bank. Florence, a born-again Christian, planned to train for missionary work in Africa. When Hazel was fifteen, Violet married and moved to a farm in the Tisdale area of Saskatchewan. Then everything changed. Florence took sick with typhoid fever and suddenly died. Hazel was devastated! When the pastor came to comfort the family, Hazel was nowhere to be found. She didn't answer their calls. Soon everyone was looking for her. Filled with sorrow, guilt and remorse, Hazel was hiding under the stairway.

"Florence is in Heaven," the pastor said when he found her hiding place. That did not ease Hazel's guilty soul. Then he wisely asked Hazel if she was ready to go to heaven if she, herself, died. In gasping sobs Hazel told him about stealing money from God and from Florence.

"Jesus died for your sins," the godly man reminded Hazel. "He still offers forgiveness if you confess your sins."

"Right then I prayed and asked for forgiveness," Hazel states, "and peace came back to my heart, knowing that I was forgiven. I was already fifteen years old. Thinking back on this event, I am surprised that I should have been so wicked."

Florence had been teaching a Sunday school class of girls. The pastor now asked Hazel to teach the class. With mixed emotions she took the place of her sister, whose death had brought Hazel back into fellowship with God. It was difficult. She was hardly older than the students.

"Why don't you gather children from the neighbourhood and bring them to Sunday school?" the superintendent suggested some time later. "You could start a new class of your own." So during the week she visited homes, asking if she could take their children to Sunday school. She often had as many as ten kindergarten and grade one children in her class. She wanted them to know Jesus.

All through high school Hazel was eagerly waiting to prepare for missionary work. In 1934 at age sixteen, she graduated from grade twelve with honours and one extra subject counting toward her first year in University. The future lay before her, bright and beckoning. But by now her mother was bedridden. The family felt Hazel should stay home to care for her. Reluctantly, Hazel submitted to their wishes. She was only sixteen. Hazel continued to do the housework, the canning, and the baking. Not entirely confined to the house, Hazel joined a group of young Bridge players. She and her partner won prize after prize. Every prize pulled Hazel deeper into what was becoming an addictive habit. Finally, Hazel knelt before the Lord once again, vowing to use her time to glorify Him. Her card-playing days were over.

"More protein might help your wife," the doctor told Mr. Page. It was an expense they could not afford, but they prayed and the Lord provided in an amazing way. Looking out her window that day, Hazel's mother saw a duck flopping around in the ditch across the road. Hazel caught, killed, dressed and cooked it. Over the next few days, with the added protein, Mrs. Page improved. Hazel had learned a valuable lesson about prayer and the Lord's provision.

Hazel worked hard at home, but she also took any courses she thought would be useful for missionary work, like Hawaiian guitar lessons. Her pastor tutored her through the Preliminary Teacher Training Course of the Moody Bible Institute, of which he was an alumnus.

In January Hazel wrote in her diary that her mother's health seemed to improve. "Mother's last scab came off, back healing fine too. (Shingles?)" But in March, her mother was again taken to the doctor, this time with a bad case of hives. Several times Hazel recorded that her mother was cross. "Once she told me I was running down my health by going to so many meetings." But Hazel and her mother also had wonderful times reading Scripture and praying together.

For three years Hazel remained at home. Then in 1937, a missionary, speaking at their young peoples' meeting, told about all the excuses she once used to avoid God's call to China. Hazel listened, guilt-ridden. God met her that day and she vowed to begin preparing to go to China.

# CHAPTER 3

## STRATEGIC EDUCATION

Hazel enrolled at Saskatoon Bible College and soaked up all the Bible knowledge she could. Of special interest were the speakers, missionaries from the far corners of the earth. For the first two years of Bible College, she rode back and forth to school on her bike, but the last year she lived away from home for the first time. This was Hazel's final year at Saskatoon Bible College, and dormitory life was something new for her. "It was God's grace that provided all I needed," she stated.

Hazel looked at herself in the mirror with delight. She adjusted the gold lace collar that perfectly complemented the gold beading on the front and sleeves of her navy blue dress. The Lord had provided much more than she had expected. Almost ready now for her graduation banquet, she placed her new wine-coloured hat on her head, tucking in a few stray wisps of hair. From the top of her head to the white shoes on her feet, everything was new. Never before in her life had she felt so blessed. The Lord had even supplied money for a school pin, her diploma and several other little necessities. The banquet (catered by the Intermediate Class), and the graduation itself, were milestones in many ways. But for Hazel the highlight of the weekend was the Bible College Missionary Conference. As she listened to compelling stories from places like China, Africa and Japan, Hazel was really hearing only one word: "Go!" She was trying. With every fibre of her being, she was trying.

She had been in contact with The China Inland Mission and had learned that all correspondence—including her personal résumé, doctrinal statements, medical papers, six references and a signed mission statement—should be finished by the end of April if she was to be considered as a 1940 candidate. Being a meticulous person, Hazel took days to record her belief on the condition of the heathen. She made the deadline, then eagerly watched the mail for a reply. When the letter arrived, she quickly opened it and scanned the words. The news was disappointing. Because of the war (WWII), she would not be able to go to China for at least a year. A letter from Mr. Glover, Director of the China Inland Mission (CIM) for America, followed in June. "The men who applied that year and the ladies who had been ready to go for the past two years, would sail in the fall." Hazel would be included in the next group. Once again she was waiting.

Because of the war, jobs were plentiful. She got a job at the Dairy Pool, where she weighed and crated eggs to be shipped down East and to England for the soldiers. Thirty-five workers processed eight carloads of four hundred cases of eggs in eight days. Hazel made $19.00. She had lots of time to think as she worked and finally made a decision. She would step out in faith and teach Summer Bible School. Hazel teamed up with Myrtle Nichols to teach in three districts not far from Saskatoon. In a flurry of preparation, she mended and patched, sewed a dress for her mother, and a dress, two aprons and a nightgown for herself.

The girls arrived at their first stop, Wurtzburg School, with four suitcases, Hazel's guitar, a big bag of bedding and their Bibles. They took part in a two-hour service. From there they went to the Chalmers' home where they unloaded their luggage and were just in time to sing and give an object lesson at another two-hour service. All that before they even unpacked. The summer was off to a fast start. Their schedule was to teach in one area for two weeks, visit the home of every child registered and close with a *demonstration program*. They had no vehicle and the homes were quite scattered.

Hazel estimated that they walked forty-three miles those first two weeks. Of course, the idea wasn't just to visit, but to present the Gospel in every home as well.

At the next location, Neuhoffnung School, a bed and stove were provided so that they could sleep, cook and teach in the school. The families generously provided food, and the absent schoolteacher told them to help themselves to his garden. Again they visited every home in the district, leaving literature at each one. At Langham they had over sixty on the roll and as many as fifty-two attending at one time. That large enrolment added hours onto the time needed to call on all the parents. Hazel arrived back home the middle of August.

Then another avenue of preparation for missionary work opened up. Hazel discovered she could take medical training at Bethany Hospital, a Salvation Army maternity hospital for unmarried mothers. Time was so short that she was forced to buy ready-made uniforms.

It was September 3, 1940. The sky was dark, sprinkled with millions of stars. Hazel had just finished her first day of training and couldn't get to sleep. The lights of Saskatoon twinkled, reflecting off the few clouds that were visible. On a high hospital bed, alone in a glassed-in veranda, Hazel kept reviewing the day, keeping sleep at bay. She had arrived at the hospital at 10:00 A.M., eager to know what she would be doing and how she would like it. Major White, the matron of the hospital, helped her settle in. Because the nurse was busy in the nursery with the mothers and babies, Major White quickly assigned Hazel to her first job: wash the case room table, all the furniture and half way up the wall with a Lysol solution. It took all morning.

From then on, Hazel's first duty each day was bed baths and bedpans. Hazel was surprised to be included with the staff for morning Scripture reading and prayer. After breakfast she helped weigh and bathe from ten to sixteen babies. When the bottles arrived, the young mothers fed their babies, then talked to and played with them. Half of the girls were giving their babies up for adoption, but they were still expected to care for them until they went to their new homes.

Her next learning experience was in the delivery room. Hazel had arrived at this maternity hospital totally ignorant of the birthing process, and suddenly she was assisting in delivering babies. This was Hazel's introduction to the facts of life. After one quick lesson on giving an injection (into an orange), she was also administering painkillers under the doctor's direction.

Hazel in training at the maternity hospital.

Two unique opportunities for ministry opened there for Hazel. One was a baby boy who had been there for several months. He was cranky and no one seemed to like him. Hazel's love and attention soon had him laughing and cooing. Eventually he was adopted into a wonderful home. The second was one of Hazel's unmarried Bible school classmates, who came in as a patient. Hazel assisted in the delivery and then loved and counselled the girl to turn everything over to the Lord. The mother kept her baby, and her friendship with Hazel continued through the years.

During the winter months, when Bible College was in session, Hazel taught part-time at the college during the day and worked night duty at Bethany Hospital. Twice Hazel assisted when the doctor had to turn a baby during delivery. She filed the experience in her memory for later use. Much as she loved maternity work, it was not her career choice. So when the call came for her to attend the China Inland Mission Candidate School in Toronto, she took a break from her medical training and another giant step toward the mission field. She left Saskatoon by train on May 11, 1941.

For a girl who had grown up on the prairies, the long train trip to Toronto was quite an adventure. Hazel watched the scenery, read an entire book, ate whenever she pleased and talked with a good many people on the train. Often when she walked down the aisle to use the facilities she noticed a young man reading his Bible.

"I read my Bible, too," Hazel thought silently each time she passed him. "I'd love to tell him I'm on my way to Toronto to attend the CIM Candidate School. I wonder what he'd say if he knew I hope to go to China some day to serve the Lord." Hazel had been taught that a proper young woman never approached a man to converse with him. Being a proper young woman, Hazel kept her silence even though she itched to talk to him. For three days and three nights Hazel lived, slept and ate on the train.

*China Inland Mission.* Hazel caught sight of the sign being held up by Mr. Brownlee and Dr. Isaac Page and hurried over to meet them. The young man from the train followed her. She introduced herself and the young man introduced himself. He was Lawrence McElheran, also a missionary candidate. Mr. Brownlee and Dr. Page were still chuckling hours later. They couldn't believe that these two young people had travelled together all that way and had not spoken a word to each other.

# CHAPTER 4

## A TASTE OF LINGUISTICS

It was an enthusiastic group of candidates that sat down to their first meal together. Hazel had come prepared to do whatever she was asked to do and eat what was served to her. After all, when she became a missionary to China, she would be eating many strange things. But who would have expected milk to be served to adults? When she was a child, the family couldn't afford milk so she wasn't used to it. In fact, she detested it. Milk would not be a staple in China, would it? If drinking milk was what it would take to get to China, Hazel would drink milk.

Hazel was always conscientious and this trait applied to her chores here, too. One day, as the cook washed the dishes and the girls dried them, Hazel returned several dishes to the dishwater because there was still food on them.

"If you give me back any more dishes to wash again, I'm going to tell the leaders to send you to the Chefoo School Dormitory for missionaries' children," the cook scolded. "You'll spend your time washing dishes, doing laundry, mending the children's clothes, folding them and putting them away." She obviously thought Hazel would not want to look after children when she could be preaching the Gospel.

The six weeks' study of Chinese radicals and phonetics especially pleased Hazel. Always fluent in languages, she found this exciting. She absorbed information about Chinese customs, learned new teaching methods and new exciting things from God's Word.

"You can travel an hour or more by street car using the one fare," she wrote home, enthralled with Toronto. "I have not seen half of the city, as you well may guess." She had never lived in a place so huge that you could go in one direction for an hour and never leave the city limits. Each student was assigned to a church to teach Sunday school, give their testimony and get to know the people. Hazel rode a streetcar to her assignment, dropping in ten cents each way. Her job weighing eggs had provided for her ticket to Toronto. By careful calculation, Hazel knew that she also had streetcar fare for all except the last Sunday. She was short one thin dime. Always independent, Hazel told Mrs. Bromley, their supervisor, that she would be late for lunch that day, since she would be walking home. Mrs. Bromley guessed the reason and gave Hazel a dime for the return trip. The woman thought about this all night. If Hazel didn't have a dime for streetcar fare, she probably didn't have money to return home either.

"What are your plans for returning home to Saskatoon?" Mrs. Bromley asked Hazel the next morning.

"I don't know what I'll do," Hazel answered truthfully, "but I know the Lord will provide." He did! Mrs. Bromley asked Hazel to stay an extra month to work during the housekeeper's holiday. Without hesitation Hazel agreed.

Their course done, each candidate was now scheduled to go before the council to see if he or she would be approved for China. Hazel was sick. She had pains in her stomach and her head was swimming. What a horrible time to be sick. Finally she went to bed. One of the older girls had watched Hazel become more and more apprehensive about the upcoming interview. Now she paid Hazel a visit.

"Have you considered that this might be an attack by Satan?" the older girl asked. Hazel had not thought of that, but she was willing to admit that it could be. They prayed together and at once Hazel's head cleared and the pain in her stomach vanished. The next day Hazel stood before the council and was accepted to go to China. She was ecstatic!

The candidates scattered to their homes, to camps, and to various ministries, but Hazel remained at the CIM headquarters and looked after thirteen guestrooms, five bathrooms and the sewing room. Her muscles got a real workout, but Hazel didn't mind. This was the Lord's provision. Much to her surprise, the Lord threw in an extra blessing, summed up in a letter to her sister, Vi.

"I had the thrill of a lifetime. We, that is the cook, Evelyn Libby, a friend in Toronto and myself, set off about 2:00 P.M. in the cook's car for Niagara Falls. We passed through Hull, Grimsby, Hamilton and several other places. Grapevines and apple, plum, pear and peach trees were in abundance. What amused me as well as thrilled me was the winding road. We travelled all the way on the Queen Elizabeth Highway, which is paved with cement and lighted by electricity. You would be surprised at the curves in the roads. They were hardly straight for more than two or three miles in a stretch. The soil is very rocky and so instead of cutting through a low hill or even going over it, they would go around. When we came to the Falls, words could not express the sight. The roar of the waters is continuous and the foam rises high in the air. It seems as if there is a dark deep space behind the waters as they fall and then the sun strikes them and they show up the more beautiful because of it. We stood and looked at them for ever so long. You might be interested to know that when I was a teenager, I always said that if I got married I wanted to go to Niagara Falls on my honeymoon. So, after I enjoyed the falls, I was contented to think that I didn't need to get married because I already had my desire to see Niagara Falls fulfilled!"

Three hours after she arrived back in Saskatoon, Hazel received a call from Bethany Hospital, and the next day she was at work again, gradually settling into the routine of teaching and working. When a chance became available to help in the college printing press, she knew it was another experience she might use in missionary work. Using individual steel case letters, Hazel painstakingly set up and prepared pages for printing. It was a noisy, busy place.

The press was clanging, the gears whirling and grinding. At first no one even heard the human screams above the ear-splitting noise of the press. By the time the machinery was stopped, the gears had badly crushed Evelyn Jasper's right hand. Two fingers had to be amputated, and she was in the hospital for ten days. Everyone stepped in to fill the gap. Hazel added proofreading to what she was already doing. There was a mountain of printing to be done before graduation and conference. Conscious of finishing each job on time, Hazel enlisted people to work overtime. This brought about John Malic's joking comment that "Hazel drives like Jehu." She could relax later. Right now she would see that the job got done, and done properly.

Summer stretched out before her, and Hazel was eager to see Vi's twin boys, born June 5. As usual she didn't have money for bus fare. Why couldn't she and Ruth Bryant ride their bikes? The girls cycled from Saskatoon to Violet's farm home, seven miles from Lac Vert. Hazel was able to ooh and aah over her new nephews. The trip home was another story. Stiff head winds and rain slowed them until they had to camp for the night. The second day they continued to struggle against the wind, finally taking refuge in a farmhouse. Their hostess graciously gave them a hot supper, a warm bed and a hot breakfast in the morning, plus lunch to take with them. When the trip was finished, they were amazed to find that they had travelled 375 miles, spent only $1.30 between them and had no bicycle trouble.

Hazel's mother was still not well, suffering from neuralgia and often put on complete bed rest. For years Hazel had been available to help her mother. Would she be needed at home another year, or two or three? She prayed.

"If you don't get your wife out of Saskatchewan you'll lose her," the doctor informed Mr. Page. "I suggest you move to British Columbia; perhaps the change in climate will be good for her." It was worth a try. They packed things to be shipped if they decided to stay, and Hazel's parents headed west. By the time they reached Alberta, Mrs. Page was feeling better. After several weeks at the coast she felt quite well, so they spent the winter of 1942-43 in Victoria, BC.

Hazel was teaching at the Saskatoon Bible College when Mr. Herb Whealey of the Wycliffe Bible Translators presented the great need for people to train in linguistics. Hazel had learned basic linguistics at candidate school, where Mr. Raymond Frame had taught the students how to make the sounds in the Chinese language accurately. Now Hazel was captivated by the phonetic possibilities, enabling one to write down, reproduce and analyse the sounds of any language. Even more exciting was the ability to translate God's Word into that language. Mr. Whealey, from People's Church in Toronto, made a statement that intrigued her. "Even those waiting to go to other countries should take this training in preparation for their work." How could she not respond? She enjoyed languages and had learned French, Latin and some German without much trouble. Hazel was also interested to know that People's Church had made an agreement with Wycliffe. They would take on fifty dollars a month of support for any missionary candidate who took the linguistic training and went to the mission field.

"Summer Institute of Linguistics (SIL) would be good training for future missionary work," Hazel reasoned. "If the Lord will supply a job so I can pay the fees, I'll go." So Hazel signed up to take a thirteen-week linguistics course in Bacone, Oklahoma, that summer of 1943. Then she prayed that needed finances would be provided. When Hazel prayed for finances she always looked to the Lord for ways to earn the money herself. The Lord answered two prayers at once.

Her parents decided to stay in British Columbia. Hazel's mother was now well enough to do without her help. But now Hazel had the huge job of selling her parents' house and many of their household items. Hazel's parents hired her to help crate and ship their belongings and paid her what they would have paid an outsider to do the job. In a bold move, Hazel asked her parents to cash in a life insurance policy they had taken out for her. That policy had come at great sacrifice to her parents and they were reluctant to agree. Finally they gave in. Supplied with a scholarship and the money from her parents, Hazel packed up and booked her train trip, to Oklahoma.

You could travel anywhere by rail for a set fee as long as you didn't retrace any part of the trip, so Hazel first went to Victoria to spend a few days with her parents. Next she travelled to Los Angeles, where she visited churches and toured interesting places, carrying her suitcase, guitar and purse everywhere she went. Then she went on to Oklahoma. When she arrived there, her suitcase was not on the train with her. Regretfully, she had to spend some of her hard-earned money for a change of clothes, while her case was located.

Hazel loved the courses in linguistics. Several weeks into their course the students were given their first test, a "Seashore Test" that involved tone, length and stress. Hazel was not concerned, expecting to do as well as she had with French and Latin. Her mark, however, was very low.

"We'll let you write the test again," Dr. Kenneth L. Pike told Hazel. "Perhaps you were nervous and that affected your mark." One of the instructors, Dr. Pike, had a soft spot for Hazel and her determination to go to China. Poor health had previously prevented him from going to China.

Hazel was confident she would do well this time. She didn't. Again she got a low mark. "I'm sorry, Hazel," Dr. Pike stated. "The test indicates there is no way you would be able to learn the tonal language of China."

# CHAPTER 5

## MEXICO

Hazel was confused. Had she made a mistake? Had she heard wrong? Had she been so enthralled with the pictures of China that it was only her own desire? Why did she do so poorly on this test when she learned other languages so easily? Was God closing the door to China? Why had God given her such a burden for China if she couldn't go there? Questions flooded her mind. Hazel knew one thing. The Lord had called her into His work. If the door to China closed, she would find another place to serve Him!

Dr. Pike saw her disappointment. He also saw her missionary heart and her love for the Lord. He decided to try one more test. In Dr. Pike's office for almost an hour, he and his sister, Eunice, took turns saying things in tonal languages, asking Hazel to repeat them.

"Hazel, go to China," Dr. Pike finally said with a smile. "You won't learn Chinese by recognizing whether the tones are high, low or medium, but by imitating what you hear. You have made only five minor errors during this whole time of repeating after us. You'll learn to speak good Chinese." Hazel was a natural mimic. She chuckled inside remembering the many times she and her brother John had mimicked people, and been scolded.

Of course, she couldn't go to China. World War II was raging. That door was closed, but the door for service in Mexico was wide open. With the promise of $50.00 a month from the People's Church in Toronto, Hazel applied to go to

Mexico with Wycliffe Bible Translators, trusting the Lord to supply her needs. Miraculously, a gift arrived to cover the travel expenses of all the workers going to the headquarters of SIL in Mexico City. Hazel was finally on her way to the mission field.

The Wycliffe Bible Translator's Conference was held in Palmira, Mexico. Hazel heard countless stories about the Lord's work in Mexico and received her assignment. She was teamed up with Joyce Jenkins from the USA, to work among the thousands of Otomi Indians in the province of Hidalgo, north of Mexico City. Joyce was a bit older than Hazel and already knew some Spanish. A train took them part way, and then they spent the night in an inn. There was no secure lock, so when men knocked on the door the girls barricaded it with all the furniture and spent a very nervous night.

They were more than ready when Wycliffe missionaries Bethel Bower and Dorothy Wright arrived from Huehuetla with hired men and donkeys. Their baggage was loaded onto the pack animals and Hazel climbed onto her donkey. This would probably be no different from riding a horse when she was a child. Nothing turned out to be the same. First of all, the stirrups were about four inches too short.

Hazel recalls, "It wasn't too bad when I could hang my legs but it almost broke my legs when I had to use them (the stirrups) going down hill. I got so tired bumping up and down that I could not hold back the tears. I was so glad when we could stop for a minute to get our third bite to eat and change mules again." The fact was, she had never ridden any animal for ten hours and consequently, she was very relieved to arrive at their first night's stop at dusk. The next day they went on to Huehuetla where they stayed several days with Bethel and Dorothy.

Hazel was impressed with Bethel and Dorothy, both graduates of the Bible Institute of Los Angeles (BIOLA). Hazel saw in them the type of missionary she wanted to be. They carried water and wood, ground corn and made tortillas. Hazel learned by experience not to look down at the path with a jar of water on her head!

Hazel had her first opportunity to work alongside the people. It was coffee country. Coffee beans were spread all over to dry in the sun, and the roasting and grinding process was in full swing. Hazel crossed a river on a narrow, slanted pole bridge and hiked up a mountain to pick coffee beans with the people. She and Bethel together netted only as much that day as one native person would in half a day.

Finally, the second week in January 1944, Hazel and Joyce were on their way to their very own place of ministry, San Gregorio. Hazel wrote about the house that had been rented for them. "With no furniture and dirt floors, it was a challenge to our ingenuity." Huge spiders, as large as Hazel's hand, clung to the walls, and fleas were everywhere. When the fleas were especially troublesome, one man jokingly suggested they invite all their friends over. "Then," he added, "when they leave, hopefully they'll take the fleas with them." Later they rented the middle room of the municipal building, with the jail on one side and an unfinished schoolroom on the other. It was fine except when the jail was full of noisy men.

Don Rafael was assigned to work as their informant as they learned the Otomi language. He was gentle, kind and a natural teacher.

"We can hold his nose to confirm a nasalization or a vowel; hold a paper in front of his mouth to see if a 'K' has an aspiration or is unaspirated; even look down his throat to see if there is an X or a glottal stop. It is really fun." When the girls began forming sentences by themselves, Don Rafael's eyes danced, and when Hazel told him they were going to translate the Bible into Otomi, his whole face lit up. To reduce the Otomi language, or any language to writing, meant using the trade language (Spanish), as well as the tribal language (Otomi). They asked question after question of people who knew both languages. What is this? What am I doing? Please say it again. Did I say it right? The answers were written down with a guess at what each actually meant. Words or phrases they heard in conversation were jotted down so they could ask Don Rafael the meanings and their use in sentences. Joyce, knowing Spanish, was able to keep the Otomi and Spanish separate, but Hazel had to write everything phonetically. Then, not wanting to trouble Joyce, she looked up the words in a Spanish-English dictionary. If it was not Spanish and not English, it was Otomi. Hazel learned Spanish and Otomi at the same time—it was a challenge she enjoyed.

There was nothing written down in Otomi, so Hazel and Joyce worked together to reduce the language to writing, first developing an alphabet with the least number of letters. They were *eyes deep* in learning the language and often had what Hazel referred to as their *angelic host* watching (children who loved to watch them study). Peering over the half-wall, the children were intrigued with the bright Coleman gas lamp and bold enough to complain when the lamp smoke bothered their eyes. They also loved to watch the typewriter work and listen to the radio, which was on for a little while each day. Hazel began giving the boys paper and pencil so they could copy words. They did such a meticulous job that one copied a complete sentence upside down.

Cooking meals and doing laundry was taking up time they wanted to spend learning the language. The girls asked for someone to "work for them," and an entire family moved in: a widow, Dona Maria, her twelve-year-old son, Basiyo, and eight-year-old Rosita. This gave the girls more time for language study and firsthand acquaintance with the customs of the people, including hens running in and out of the house and roosting in the corners.

Hazel's first experience at a local funeral saddened her heart. The wee baby lay on a table in a bed of flowers in the middle of the house, with candles near the head of the child. Musicians played outside the door. The women in the funeral procession carried candles to light the child's soul into the next world. Food and money were put into the coffin for the spirit's use in the world beyond. Hazel yearned to tell them about the hope Christ gives, but didn't have the words yet.

There seemed to be no end to the medical work. Loss of life appalled Hazel and Joyce, especially when it was the result of ignorance and superstition. One day a man came with a terrible foot infection from stepping on a thorn. Twice a day Hazel tended to his foot. One day she went to his home and found the witch doctor, with his paraphernalia spread out, in the process of performing his witchcraft. The man of the house told him to pack up his paper dollies and marigolds and incense. The witch doctor packed up but he didn't leave. He stayed to watch as Hazel carried on her medical work. He tasted the Epsom salts she put in the basin to soak the foot. Then he sat and nodded approval.

Hazel and Joyce in Mexico

Because China still had first place in Hazel's heart, the partnership with Joyce would never be permanent. Different personalities and learning styles also caused difficulties. They worked together, but there was an underlying friction. Joyce wanted someone who would stay. Hazel was waiting for China to open. In March 1944, Hazel was excited to hear that some workers were being allowed to return to China.

# CHAPTER 6

## READING CAMPAIGN

Hazel had ample opportunity to be in the local homes, simply four walls, a door, perhaps a window and a thatched roof. A box on the wall was always decorated as an altar, with pictures of the Virgin Mary. A few boards across the rafters, and various hanging bags provided storage. Shelves held their few dishes and water pots. A pile of stones and mud made up their stove. At times coffee beans were heaped everywhere. A few low stools and perhaps a chest were the extent of their furniture, with straw mats rolled up in the corner to sleep on. Hazel couldn't help but contrast this lifestyle with what she had left behind in Canada.

The house the girls lived in was much better than what the people lived in. Then the rains came. Drip! Drip! Drip! Water leaked in all over the place until the girls finally had their beds together and Joyce's *manga* (a big rubber poncho worn on muleback) over them. Joyce still had to sleep under her umbrella. Don Rafael advised them to withhold the rent until the roof was fixed. They did and it was!

Six months after arriving in San Gregorio, and with more than 1000 words recorded in the Otomi language, Joyce went to work at Camp Wycliffe. Hazel was reassigned to help Hazel Spotts among the Mazahua Indians (related to the Otomi). It was hard to say good-bye to the folks in San Gregorio, but even that was easier than the ten-hour return trip on the back of a mule. Mildred Kiemele, Hazel Spotts' co-worker, was going on furlough and mission policy didn't allow single girls to be alone. At least the fleas were not a problem in San Miguel—never in bed. "They can't find breeding places in cement like they do in dirt. What a happy release from the scratching."

The Lord had another reason for placing Hazel Page in the Mazahua area. A Mazahua tribal woman had lost her first three babies at birth, each after a difficult breech delivery. Maybe Hazel could help. While she waited for the breech baby to arrive, Hazel delivered another baby. No bed, only rags, but mother and baby girl were fine. They paid her with a chicken and some corn. As the time for the high-risk delivery approached, Hazel wondered if she would really be able to help. The two times she had watched the doctor manually turn a baby in the womb at Bethany Hospital was not much training. Could she do it herself? Would this baby even need to be turned? It did! Calling on the Lord for wisdom and strength, Hazel turned the baby. The mother wept with joy as she held her first living baby.

Hazel Spotts and Mildred had been working on a Mazahua hymnbook, aiming to have it printed before Mildred left for furlough. Enter Hazel Page with printing experience, just at the right time. The printing press in Mexico City wasn't quite the same as in Saskatoon, though. First the press had to be cleaned and repaired. Certain linotype letters had to be purchased to complete the alphabet, since Mazahua had fourteen vowel sounds. It took several days just to find and buy supplies like paper, covers, and rulers, and it was two weeks before printing began. Each page had to be printed twice: once with plain vowels, the second time to add dots over some vowels and lines over others.

"We found Hazel Page and Hazel Spotts in a tiny room, … on the top floor of the National Museum, printing the hymn book…," someone wrote in a letter. "It was fun to meet Hazel Page. She has a wholesomeness, coupled with a putting of her work before self, which makes us have a deep respect and love for her and her work."

"Today we put almost 1700 sections of our book together," Hazel's letter stated. "Each section has four sheets folded in half and they have to be slipped inside each other. I am enjoying it—making it a game by counting backwards, forwards, by twos, etc. Then I time myself to see how many I can get done in five minutes. Then I see if I can do more than Hazel does. It is quite a big job handling papers all day but it is ... a thrill to see the book ... getting that much nearer to being finished." The total project took three months. Hazel found it comforting to know the Lord would use every past experience. There was now a hymnbook in Mazahua.

When Lydia Zinke, a graduate of Moody Bible Institute, arrived, she was also hoping to go to China some day. The Mission decided to send Lydia and Hazel Page to learn a tonal language. It would be good preparation for the study of Chinese, which is also tonal. They began in Mexico City, studying a dialect of Mixteco, with Señor Venancio David Aquino. He was well educated and knew both Spanish and Mixteco. Lydia had never learned a foreign language before and found it hard to remember the words, but got the tones quickly. Hazel, on the other hand, learned the words quickly but was slower in getting the tones. Their mutual interest in China drew them together in prayer. Finally, in December 1944 they moved to Tetelcingo into Mr. and Mrs. Pittman's large house right on the highway. For two weeks they were alone there, enjoying separate bedrooms, Lydia downstairs and Hazel upstairs.

Hazel had a dream one night, rather a nightmare, of men coming up the stairs after her. Why would she have such a silly dream? Then, one night sometime later, Hazel was sleeping soundly when something woke her. It was 1:30 in the morning. Was this another dream? The head and shoulders of a man appeared in the dim light. Hazel went toward him, fists ready to knock him down the stairs, but he was already up and another man followed. Hazel hit the first one, making him stumble. This was no dream. She had hit solid flesh! One of the men grabbed Hazel by the neck.

Screaming, Hazel sank to her knees asking questions between screams as the men threatened to kill her. "You cannot have me," she screamed. "I belong to God!"

"What's wrong?" Lydia called up the stairs in English.

Hazel felt a cold steel blade against her neck.

"Get help!" She yelled, just as Lydia let out a blood-curdling scream that went on and on and on. Startled, the men let Hazel go and turned to flee. Ironically, the trap door had fallen shut. With one hand Hazel lifted the door, grabbed a man by the neck and pushed him down the stairs.

Almost paralyzed with fright, the girls barricaded the kitchen door and huddled under the table hoping help would come. No one came. A neighbour did come but found the house dark and quiet. Hazel was bruised and both girls were traumatised. Days later, Hazel was able to claim II Timothy 1:7: "God hath not given us the spirit of fear; but of power, and of love, and of a sound mind." The Lord took away the fear and Hazel stayed on and continued language study. Lydia returned home. She never went to China.

In learning new languages, the International Phonetic Script is used. It has only one sound for each symbol. As material is gathered from a new language, the sounds are charted to find out which are similar and why some are different in different surroundings. Similar sounds can often be combined in one unit of speech (phonemic symbol). When all the sounds used in that language are charted, this total makes up the alphabet. Hazel was never without paper and pencil, and her attention to detail and her enthusiasm were great assets in linguistic work. She was, however, more than ready for her holiday when it came due. After a month's vacation back in Canada, she was pleased to teach Phonetics at Canadian Camp Wycliffe in Saskatchewan.

"Most of you know by now that 1945 is to be the year of the big literacy campaign all over Mexico," Dick Pittman wrote in the Wycliffe prayer letter. "The government is going to great pains to teach all Mexicans to read, and plans to teach the Indians by means of bilingual primers." It was an amazing opportunity for the mission. Not only would they cooperate in this campaign, but they also pushed to have as much reading material as possible ready as soon as possible. They purchased a little printing plant (operated in connection with the School of Anthropology), so they could print tracts, stories and primers. The Lord had set before them a wide open door, and they went through it with enthusiasm.

When Hazel returned to Mexico in September, the Government-sponsored Reading Campaign was already underway, targeting fifty tribal languages that had never been reduced to writing. The foundation was being laid for people to have the Word of God in their own language!

Hazel's partner now was Elizabeth Soney, known as *Sunny Beth*. Resident missionaries, already reducing local languages into writing, provided lists of sentences. Using these lists, the girls prepared primers for the campaign. There was no printing press available there, so the greatest tool was the hectograph. This is a flat, page-sized tin pan containing a jelly-like substance. First, using indelible ink, they would write out on paper a page of the primer. This page was laid on the hectograph and rubbed well to transfer the ink to the jelly base. That ink in turn would transfer onto every new sheet of paper placed on the jelly base. When they finished all the copies of one page, they could clean the ink off the hectograph and start over with another page. The primers were about sixty lessons long, so it was a time-consuming, tedious job. Hazel and Sunny began their first campaign among the Tseltal Indians.

Hazel chuckled over a problem she had in one of the reading campaigns. The first sentence in the primer was, "This is my foot." Whenever Hazel would read, "This is my foot," one lady would reply, "This is *your* foot." Hazel tried to explain without success. Finally the Lord gave Hazel much-needed wisdom. "The *paper says*, 'This is my foot'. Now, what does the paper say?" Hazel asked. The lady replied, "This is my foot." Problem solved! This lesson proved valuable in teaching Scripture also. "God's Word says" became a statement Hazel used often in teaching the Word of God.

Throughout the reading campaign there was evidence of a hunger and thirst for the things of God, so portions of Scripture were also shared with the people. In January Sunny Beth and Hazel went to Chiapas where Ruth Hitchner worked with the Ch'ol Indians. In March they were in Tabasco among the Chontal Indians helping Kathryn Keller and Margaret Harris. Altogether, Hazel was exposed to ten tribal languages in Mexico: Otomi, Tepehua, Mixteco, Aztec, Popoluca, Tseltal, Chol, Chontal, Mazahua and Zapateco, plus Spanish and English. "It was like 'tasting' them, not really being fluent in them or making them a part of my life," she recalls. Hazel enjoyed the villages. Only in these outlying areas could Hazel see things like the buzzard. "The buzzard is the most homely big black bird I ever saw. He eats refuse (human and otherwise), and walks in a sneaking manner. He loves to spread his wings in the sun as he stands on the ground and also loves to sit up in an old bare tree."

When summer arrived again, Hazel was back in Canada at the Canadian Summer Institute of Linguistics. She took some classes, filled a few speaking engagements and visited with her brothers Irvine and John, and her sister Violet. During Hazel's time in Canada, Violet was put on complete bed rest. Hazel was stunned when Vi asked her if she could come and help her. Much as she wanted to help her sister, the Lord's call on her life could not be ignored. To Vi she wrote: "The China Inland Mission advised me to go to Mexico again … as it may be only a few months until … the time actually comes for me to go to China." In a bold step of faith, Hazel went to Saskatoon and packed in preparation for China. Then she returned to Mexico.

Rev. Oswald J. Smith and his wife from People's Church in Toronto visited Hazel in Mexico. Their church was Hazel's most faithful supporting church. There were still at least eight places waiting for the Reading Campaign. In each of these, missionaries had roughed out a primer and other reading materials. Hazel and Sunny Beth were partners again. This time they were well stocked with supplies: paper of all kinds, crayons, paints, rulers, pens and ink, paste, paper clips, matching games, Lotto and Parcheesi, even magic slates. All this was added to the bedding and personal possessions they would need for six or seven months, and carted from place to place by mule or burro.

They started at Tuxla. They would first gather the children and teach them the words of the primer, using flash cards. When the children had learned all of the words, the primer would be brought out. It wouldn't take long before they realised that the words they were reading made sense. New words appeared with each new page. With this teaching method the missionaries went from one hut to another. Many adults had been told that they were ignorant and believed they could never learn to read, but they loved the pictures. It was not hard to get them to learn the word under each picture. Suddenly the adults would realise they were reading. Eyes glowed as people who never had a lesson in school learned to read.

Unbeknown to Hazel, a letter, written by Mr. Townsend, the founder and director of Wycliffe Bible Translators, was on its way to Mr. Herbert Griffin of CIM. Written from their Jungle Training Camp where Hazel was helping conduct reading classes, Mr. Townsend made suggestions regarding Hazel's future with CIM.

"Miss Hazel Page, an accepted candidate of yours … is hoping that you may be able to send her out to China. We can recommend her most highly … Hazel has a very good disposition, has all-around ability. (You should see the electric game she arranged for the team to help with reading classes.) She takes to pioneering very well, and if you would permit me to make a recommendation it would be that she be assigned to one of the tribes that does not yet have the New Testament in its language."

Mr. W.C. Townsend

"Dear Miss Page," began a letter to Hazel from CIM.

"Just a note to see if you would be in a position to come to Philadelphia next month. We are expected to send one or two candidates to Missionary Conference and your name has come to my mind. Then there is the thought that you might, when we have a group of candidates in the Mission home under training, give them help in linguistics."

Herbert M. Griffin, CIM

A telegram from CIM followed. Hazel was out in the tribal regions and with no way to contact her on short notice, Mr. Townsend replied on her behalf. She was needed to finish the campaign in Tabasco and then was free to go, he explained. Hazel knew nothing about this until days after she was expected in Philadelphia.

The village of Tabasco was the last stop for their campaign. Hazel had often seen the comic strip featuring *Maggie and Jiggs,* so she was amused when she saw the married women in Tabasco with their hair tightly wound up in the shape of a handle. It had never occurred to her that there was a place where women actually wore their hair like Maggie's. Others wore theirs in a thick braid dangling down their bare brown backs. This was an industrious group. Singer Sewing Machines hummed at all hours of the day making palm hats. Then the hats were polished with sulfur powder, pressed on a special machine in one of the buildings and shipped or taken out for sale. Spanish was the trade language, and the people saw no need to learn the local language. Hazel's contribution to the reading campaign was done. Her work in Mexico was finished, but it had laid a solid foundation for her future work. Hazel was headed for China.

# CHAPTER 7

## CHINA AT LAST

*Excited* might be too calm a word to explain Hazel's feelings about finally being at Candidate School. She was one of eighteen at the China Inland Mission Home in Philadelphia, hoping to sail to China that fall. For six weeks the candidates studied the history of the Mission, the history of the Chinese language and the Chinese people. Then thirteen left for Briercrest, Saskatchewan, to attend the Summer Institute of Linguistics and some went home. Hazel did deputation work, went sightseeing in New York, visited friends and relatives in Ontario and for two weeks helped with tent meetings in Chicago. When she headed west on July 19, she again made use of a ticket that allowed her to go wherever she wanted as long as she didn't backtrack. For almost a month she visited as many people as she could, even if only for a few hours. She was building a strong prayer base for her future missionary work. She then had three months to spend with her parents, unpack, answer letters and repack for China. The Mission supplied an extensive outfit list:

Eiderdown, pillows, 2 or 3 blankets, steamer rug, bedspread, two flannelette blankets, sheets, white pillow cases (coloured for travelling), bath towels, face towels, tablecloths and luncheon cloths, tray cloths or doilies, table napkins, dusters, tea towels, one thick dressing gown (all wool, light weight), one thin dressing gown, slips (shadow proof), long-sleeved cotton gowns or pyjamas, thinner ones for summer, woollen union suits (knee length, long sleeves), lighter weight suits for spring and autumn.

Thin vests, white or colored bloomers, woven or knitted bloomers, sport length bloomers (below knees, dark) cholera belts, woven or made of flannel (worn around the kidney area), thick woollen stockings, medium woollen stockings, white stockings, colored stockings. Warm dresses, pullover sweaters, colored voile or gingham dresses. Necks not too low, sleeves just above elbow, skirts not more than eleven inches from floor, warm thick coat, waterproof coat, woollen sweater, warm gloves, soft felt hat for winter, cotton hats with wide brim, red cloth for hat linings (to protect from the sun). One pair wristlets to knuckles, dark glasses, white shoes for summer, shoes with rubber heels, long gaiters (covering for the lower leg), rubbers, rubber apron, lengths of material for foreign or Chinese dress. That list covered the linens and clothing she would need.

Then there were household items. Alcohol stove, tools, combination set (screwdriver, etc.), good hammer, hanging looking glass (mirror), small tea kettle, teapot, coffee pot, candlestick, saucepan, funnel, hot water bottle, bedpan and enema, knives, forks and spoons (initialled), salt and pepper shakers, drinking glasses, cups and saucers, shoe-blacking outfit, simple medicines, vases, pictures, books, stationery, exercise books, sewing basket and notions, soap (toilet and laundry). Extra nice to have, camp bed and mattress. Trunks not too large or too heavy. Too much pink or red not good colors for China. She questioned some of the list, but packed it all anyway. Her father was a great help, putting dividers in her trunk so she could use it later as a cupboard, initialling her silverware, choosing her tools. Her mother insisted a small kettle would not do. Hazel left with a good-sized teakettle!

The list continued. To be procured in Shanghai—10 yards mosquito netting, quinine, insect powder, enamelware, thin cotton mattress, oil sheet and matting. Only one box of her supplies would be taken to language school: all warm bedding, warm clothing, hot water bottle, personal household

47

items, one tin biscuits, stationery, exercise books, all books needed for first section, Chinese NT and Hymn Book. Looking over that list, Hazel could almost guess what the weather would be like at language school!

Hazel was one of forty China Inland Mission (CIM) workers and children sailing on the *SS Marine Lynx* in November. This included eighteen newly accepted candidates. Now that the war was over, General McArthur took great pains to make troop ships available to transport missionaries to that part of the world. Hazel was not the only single Canadian girl that headed for China. Edith Broadfoot from Vancouver, Eileen Singleton from Ottawa, Alberta Davis from Wainright, Alberta, Doris Leonard from Toronto, and Hazel Page from Victoria would forge a bond on that trip that would last for more than fifty years.

Hazel and Peggy Ashby seemed to be the only ones left standing as, one by one, seasick adults took to their beds. The two girls tried hard to think of something for the sixteen children to do each day. Being a war ship, *The Marine Lynx* had huge tubes running from deck to deck, and the children loved to slide down these hatches. Only the Lord prevented them from ending up in the ocean. Having sixteen children running everywhere and sliding from deck to deck was a new and frustrating experience for the crew. Since Hazel had spent the past four years in Mexico teaching children to read, she was able to come up with many interesting things to keep them occupied.

The meals were wonderful. Only once did Hazel leave anything on her tray. That was an eggplant, "cooked in a peculiar manner I had never been privileged to try before," Hazel tactfully stated. The passengers were quite a mixed bunch also, even among the missionaries. "I would think that about half of them are modern in their way of interpreting the Bible," she wrote home, "and that they were going to China more to give them (the Chinese) social teaching than to tell them of Christ." Hazel was evangelical to the bone and going to China with one purpose in mind—to proclaim Christ! The

CIM had Bible study and prayer each morning and services each evening.

Hazel was sometimes surprised when she fell asleep, sitting in a deck chair. The ocean seemed to invite sleep and increase her appetite. Hazel loved chocolate, so when she found a place that sold candy bars and soft drinks she bought a whole box of Hershey bars with almonds. Hazel enjoyed her first voyage. She never tired of watching the crew do their drill, don their life belts, man their stations, unroll the hose and send water into the ocean. The ship's hospital was busy with so many seasick plus four cases of mumps and a case of chicken pox among the CIM folk. Alberta Davis, in isolation with the mumps, received the sad news that her mother had passed away.

Shortly before midnight on December 31, 1945, the ship dropped anchor in the mouth of the Hwang Pu River. Hazel was itching to set foot in China, but they didn't start moving again until the tide changed, about nine o'clock the next morning. Customs and Immigration officers came on board and checked inoculation papers, so there was nothing left to do but stand and watch the scenery as the pilot boat guided them in. Hazel noticed the land seemed quite flat on both sides of the river, with factories and sawmills on one side and farms and little mud houses with thatched roofs on the other side. Some of the houses were close enough for Hazel to see children playing in the yards, and pigs and chickens running around and into the houses, like Mexico— but this was China!

The Chinese junks fascinated her. At one place they were so thick she couldn't imagine how they could move at all. "Of course, these Chinese junks are the kind of boats that many of China's people live on all their lives and never set their feet on solid ground," Hazel wrote in one letter. "One can hardly imagine a family being raised on such a small boat with all the cooking utensils they possess, the washing equipment and all and only a tiny little cover over part of the boat for protection. I laughed to see the family wash hung on a long bamboo pole sticking out from the end of the boat. They hadn't heard of Rinso or Oxydol but then the water of the river is rather murky to begin with." The patched sails on the boats reminded her of a patchwork quilt of many drab colours. Someone explained to her the big eye on each side of each boat: "If they have no eyes how can the boat see to get around?" Another detail Hazel was curious about was the single oar at the rear of each boat. She was informed that it worked like the tail of a fish.

Maps used by permission of OMF

China! Hazel was almost bursting with joy! On New Year's Day, 1946, the ship sailed into Shanghai harbour, and Hazel set foot in China for the first time. Without a doubt, the Lord had put that desire in her heart as a child and He was the one who carried it through. The pier was not very big and they were a large group disembarking. Coolies unloaded their belongings. The Baggage Committee arranged for half the group to go through Customs while the other half guarded the bags, then they switched. It would be easy for someone to make away with a suitcase or two in all the confusion. Each one set their baggage in order for the officer to examine. It was opened, peeked at and they were free to go. CIM workers welcomed them, and then they all piled into the back of a covered army truck to go to the drafty mission home. Sadly, the two adults and two children sick with the mumps were taken to hospital and missed all the scenery. Hazel was glad it was still daylight so she could see the rickshaws. Similar carts pulled by bicycles were even more numerous. Funny streetcars with two cars came clanging along the streets. Large, small, new, old and unusual cars ran in and out. It was amazing! The New Year's Eve service was underway when they arrived at the Mission Home, and each new candidate had five minutes to share his or her testimony.

Hazel felt warmly welcomed and much at home. The only candidate who had extensive linguistics training, Hazel was asked to explain the Monolingual approach to learning a language, which she had learned from Dr. Pike in Oklahoma. Then she had an even greater surprise. A woman had developed a simplified alphabet using only thirty-seven symbols. The Chinese alphabet uses two hundred or so basic Chinese characters. This simplified alphabet was a phonetic script resembling the Chinese characters, and representing every sound found in Chinese. This woman, Miss Leaman, was now living in Shanghai and was doing an adaptation. Because of her keen ear, Hazel was asked to assist in the process of adapting the phonetic script to the Ning Po dialect. Every weekday during the three weeks they were in Shanghai, Hazel went to listen to a Ning Po speaker read the

Scriptures. Her ability to hear and record the sounds phonetically was a great help. The end result, hopefully, would be to simplify the reading of the Scriptures in the Ning Po dialect. Hazel felt privileged to also meet Chinese missionary Christina Tsai, a valued counsellor and teacher, who was now bedridden. Both she and Miss Leaman were godly women with Ambassadors for Christ in the USA. All through Hazel's life these women had been the epitome of a missionary to China.

"There are now forty-two of us here and we come from ten different countries, so you can imagine the fun we are having mimicking one another's accents," Hazel wrote home. Yes, her family in Canada could imagine that! Rising time was 6:00 A.M. and classes began at 9:00 A.M. Their first week entailed two hours daily of theory and one of drilling. The following week they had one hour of theory and two of drilling in the sounds. Then they had two hours of drilling in Chinese sentences and one hour of private study.

Hazel wasn't quite sure when they would use the customary wadded garments, but they had all been measured as soon as they arrived in China. The rooms were not heated, but when the weather cooled, she was thankful for this silk quilted garment, wristlets, warm stockings and shoes. She was comfortable, even when the temperature was at the freezing point.

Each Saturday morning, someone would teach the group about their field of interest. Hazel presented the work of the Wycliffe Bible Translators in Mexico and the many languages she had helped with in the Reading Campaign. It was a wonderful way of getting to know who else was working in other parts of China. There were also daily times of prayer for the CIM family, at home and in China. Now, in this foreign country, Hazel came face to face with another aspect of the Lord's work—the power of Satan in this land. Teachers related actual situations the missionaries had come up against. The power of the Gospel to break the bonds gave Hazel even greater confidence in God. Perhaps she already knew all this, but here in China it came home with fresh impelling power. She recognised again her own helplessness to meet a similar situation in her own strength, and she cast herself anew on the Lord.

Their main reason for being here now was for language study. Missionary teachers explained the grammatical constructions of the language. Chinese teachers gave them Chinese sentences to translate and analyse, Chinese characters to write and oral speech to practice. The Chinese teachers were vital to learning everything correctly. Six hours a day, five days a week proved to be a good average for study time. Half the time was spent in class, the other half in private study. Hazel's first winter in China went by quickly, and she had managed to endure the dreaded cold.

Mr. Frame, one of their language instructors, began to talk of the summer heat. It would be difficult to study. Hazel's summers in Canada had never had a debilitating effect on her, she thought. It must be pretty bad in China. Mr. Frame arranged for the entire fifty-plus members of the school to be transported one hundred ten miles up the river to Kuling. This entailed fourteen hours on a small open launch, a night on the floor of a home in Kuikiang, a half-hour's ride by truck to the foot of the mountain, Laoshan, and then a three-hour walk up the stone stairways to their new home. Three hours going up the stairs! Everything here was up and down. It was vastly different from the prairies! The day was clear and the flowers, waterfalls, old temples and rivers shone in the distance; the entire area was everything Hazel had hoped to find in China. A short fifteen-minute walk took them to where they could watch incredible sunsets. The beauty and splendour were an ever-present reminder to Hazel of the majesty of God.

The Mission Home here had an amazing history. During the war, soldiers had occupied it. Windows were broken out, doors and floors ripped up and burned for firewood, walls broken down and some of the rooms even used to stable horses. Mr. Frame had overseen the restoration process, first repairing the high stone fence and then the house. When funds ran out, he had to return to Shanghai to petition the mission leaders for more money. One by one the rooms were finished. The first language students to arrive after the war pitched in to help. Beds, desks, chairs, dressers, washstands, clothes racks and wardrobes were all made out of logs pulled out of the Yangtze River. By the time Hazel's group arrived, the building was complete, even with electricity for evening use. Hazel's respect for Mr. Frame grew enormously with the telling of that story.

Not all was positive, however. Hazel didn't have fleas to contend with here, but mosquitoes were abundant. And there were rats. Some of the students were horrified, but to Hazel it brought back memories of hanging dead mice on Grandpa's front gate. Called to help a classmate one night, Hazel found a rat that was too fast for her, scooting over her feet and finally running through a hole in the wall. Hazel made sure that hole was covered, and they finally had peace. Writing home later, she stated, "32 rats caught since we came." Hazel learned that the rats in China were not like the rats at home. These lived almost entirely on rice and were excellent in the soup pot, adding much-needed protein to her diet. Hazel knew how important protein was, and this information she appreciated often through the coming years.

# CHAPTER 8

## PAOSHAN, CHINA

Anticipation was high. Everyone was looking forward to the arrival of Bishop Houghton, the General Director, and his wife in July. Basic language study was coming to an end, and Bishop Houghton would assign them to their new fields. Hazel wondered where she would be assigned and who would be her senior workers. Hazel completed her First-Section examinations of Chinese and now she was ready to go.

Hazel, Edith Broadfoot, and Doris Leonard were all assigned to Wuting, in Yunnan Province, where Mr. and Mrs. J.D. Harrison would be their senior workers. Hazel Waller also was there with them for a few months. Eileen Singleton, with another co-worker, was stationed further north on the east coast of China. Their stations assigned, the students left for their various fields of service by twos and threes.

Wuting is a walled city set in a beautiful valley. Within days of their arrival at Wuting, several individuals came to "the place where you can talk about the Jesus Doctrine," inquiring how to become Christians. Mr. Harrison thought it wise to start a nightly Bible class, and attendance was never less than twenty. One Sunday night there were around one hundred, so he made arrangements for the room to be enlarged. The greatest thrill for Hazel during this time was when Mr. Wang from Kunming came for a series of meetings. On the last night, fifteen men and boys professed to accept Christ as Saviour.

Every sixth day was the big market day in Wuting, and people from all the twenty or more surrounding villages would come to market with their produce to sell and to the mission compound for medicine.

Over five hundred others gathered for worship with the Big Flowery Miao Christians (a dialect of Miao people) on Harvest Festival Sunday. This was the day they brought their gifts of grain to the church as their yearly support of the pastor. Miao students from the middle school accompanied Doris, Floyd Larsen, Mr. Harrison and Hazel on a two-hour trip, to visit Sapushan. It was an uphill trip all the way, but they forgot everything else as schoolboys with banners floating in the air came marching to welcome them. The trail was lined with women and girls waiting to greet them. Hazel smiled to see the church decorated with both fall leaves and Christmas decorations but quickly sensed the presence of the Lord in their midst.

The Grahams had worked with these people until Mr. Graham died, and the people were still grieving. A young woman, baby on her back and tears streaming down her face, asked if Mrs. Graham was coming back. These dear people felt the loss greatly, and the new missionaries felt very inadequate as they faced the giant hole left by these seasoned workers.

Always conscious of the need for prayer support, Hazel printed over three hundred prayer letters on her little machine the middle of November. These she sent off to prayer supporters, for she needed prayer. She was now learning the Yunnanese dialect of Chinese. Miss Ch'en, a young lady who taught in the middle school, tutored the missionaries each afternoon. Two students from the normal school also helped them individually for half an hour each day. A young Christian man from the Tai tribe cooked for them, and another Christian helped with the housework.

Eleven different kinds of vegetables, chicken, beef, roast pork, pork ribs, rice and rice noodles overflowed the table for Hazel's first Christmas in China. New converts from a little town nearby joined the small group of Christians in

Wuting, and each person brought something for the meal. A live rooster had even been delivered a few days early. Hazel learned that in China, the more important the meal the more varieties of foods were served. Everyone left the table more than satisfied, physically and spiritually.

By April they were seeing the results of political unrest. Missionaries were being evacuated out of the north of China. Chinese Christians were suffering, and even an associate, Miss Lenell, and her Chinese co-labourer were beaten to death in the north. Hazel's heart went out to these dear people. As she wrote, "Foreigners can flee, but not the Chinese."

In May of 1948 new assignments were handed out. Hazel Waller and Doris were to remain in Wuting to work with Dr. and Mrs. Gray, who would soon arrive. Hazel and Edith were assigned to Paoshan, the most westerly station, among the tribal people. It was just the type of place Mr. Townsend, in Mexico, had suggested for Hazel. The Harrisons would be moving there as well. Hazel relished their incredible trip to Paoshan. There were high mountains to cross (one of which had seventy-two curves in the road), low plains, winding rivers, China's highest waterfall (Orange Tree Falls), caves, bamboo groves, flowers and fruit trees. Along the way they visited the Blind Girls' School, Orphanage, tribal printing press and friends in Kunming. At a leprosarium Hazel was introduced to a leper for the first time. It so impacted her that for the rest of her life she supported missions to the lepers.

"My name in Chinese means 'a well-watered apple tree' or 'a waterer of apple trees,'" Hazel wrote in a letter. "Isaiah 58:10 & 11 is the Scripture on which I base the hope of all this name implies. 'And if thou draw out thy soul to the hungry, and satisfy the afflicted soul; then shall thy light rise in obscurity, and thy darkness be as the noon day; And the Lord shall guide thee continually, and satisfy thy soul in drought, and make fat thy bones: and thou shalt be like a watered garden, and like a spring of water, whose waters fail not.'"

Hazel's small single room sparkled with her bright blue bedspread, blue and red curtains and clothes bag. Her crocheted rug and a grass mat bound with coloured scraps of material covered the rough uneven floor. How she appreciated the shelving her father had installed in her packing box. That held her clothes. Her steamer trunk, suitcases and book boxes were piled to create a desk. Chinese scrolls, pictures from home and calendars made the board walls look cheery. She still had one more thing to do to make it really feel like home. Outside, she and Edith planted phlox, stocks, sweet william and marigolds. The grounds already included honeysuckle, jasmine and thirty-three fruit trees. She had lots to write about to her father, also an avid gardener.

Hazel never failed to be amazed at the ingenuity of the Chinese language. Believed to have come into existence in the written form even before the time of Noah, their one character for the word "boat" contains the entire story of the Flood. It includes the characters for large boat, small boat, eight and mouth. Equally interesting to her was the word for "believe", made up of "man" leaning on "words."

A young leper.

Hazel and friend in China

Anna Pfautz joined their team in Paoshan. One day, Hazel and Anna walked for two and a half hours in deep mud to Ch'ing-chia Ts'un. Two Christian guides carried their bedding and materials on poles across their shoulders. The surrounding rice paddies were full of water at first, but after the sun began to dry the earth, their guides took them on narrow paths between the rice paddies. Suddenly a weak spot in the path gave way, and Hazel was wet up to one knee. She and Anna laughed so hard that Anna slipped up to her waist in water. They nicknamed each other *crane* and *duck* because one had only one foot in in the water while the other was all in the water. They had a good time. The mishap was quickly forgotten, though, when they arrived at the village.

Almost the first thing Hazel noticed was little girls with their feet bound. Years before, a Chinese woman could never hope to marry if her feet were not bound. That practice was quickly becoming a thing of the past in most places, and by the time Hazel arrived in China, the Lord had loosened their feet and set people's souls free. Many months later Hazel found an old pair of Chinese shoes in the yard, only five inches long, with a pointed, turned up toe about an inch beyond the sole. Hazel was informed that they belonged to a lady whose feet had been bound before she believed in Jesus. At one time her grandmother had feet no bigger than her ankle and needed servants to help her walk. That was sad, but Hazel had to laugh when she recalled the first pair of Chinese shoes she had made-to-order. Several people checked before they cut the sole. They couldn't believe her foot was so big!

Daily, Hazel and Anna were escorted to nearby villages to hold a service in each Christian home. The sixteen good Mandarin Chinese records were all played almost every day on Anna's phonograph. Hazel thanked the Lord for the records, as someone had once told her they pitied the people she taught to sing. Hazel knew her shortcomings and knew what the Lord had called her to do. The records were all part of His plan!

Being in China was a boon for Hazel's stamp collecting. Mr. Li was one of the men who traded stamps with her, old Chinese stamps that were hard to get even at that time. In exchange, Hazel gave him American, Canadian, and Mexican stamps.

Times were not easy financially for the missionaries. The value of the Chinese currency changed regularly. At one time it was four Chinese dollars to one U.S. dollar, and then it climbed to twelve million-to-one. Hazel's letters home were often covered with stamps—sometimes layers of them—since they could get stamps only in small denominations. Hazel saw it as a great opportunity for stamp collectors in Canada, like her nephew Philip.

A good way for missionaries to learn the language was to read the Bible in whatever language they were studying. By November of 1948, Hazel states, "I read a whole chapter in the Bible today in Chinese without a mistake. It surely is grand to realise I am making some progress."

Weddings of fellow missionaries were always an exciting affair. In January of 1949 they celebrated not one, but two weddings among their Canadian friends. Doris Leonard married Cyril Weller, and Hazel Waller married Orville Carlson. This latter marriage was cause for some laughter when Hazel Page received a greeting card with the following note: "Congratulations on your wedding which I understood would be over by now. I hope you are very happy." Hazel had a good laugh and stated, "Yes, I'm very happy anyway— even though I'm not married." Being single didn't bother Hazel. She was very independent and joked that she didn't need a husband because she had her Handy Andy. This handy 18-inch-long tool opened up, like a giant boy scout knife, to provide a saw, a hammer, pliers, wire cutter, screw driver, crowbar and an ax. Then, too, she had already been to Niagara Falls!

It wasn't long before she began writing about the Communists taking Shanghai and Nanking. "We are apparently safe from danger, so we are praying we will be able to stay here for a long time yet to preach the Gospel." She was still putting in long hours of language study every morning. Then she spent another hour or two in the afternoon learning Chinese, plus three hours with Mr. Tweddell on the Tuli language. They were seeing new converts come to the Lord on a regular basis, but learning the language was still Hazel's first priority. When she could, she also helped prepare stories for Mr. Ivan Albutt to publish.

The missionaries had grown accustomed to having armed soldiers around. Then gradually things began to escalate. The main military group moved out of the area, leaving about three hundred ill-equipped recruits. They frequently had firing practice outside the town. News reached the missionaries that Ch'angning, only forty miles south east, had fallen to the Communists, and within days sentries were challenging people in the streets. On April 11, 1949, the prison inmates were freed and the prison set on fire. The next morning there were no soldiers or police to be seen, only countrymen armed with old muskets and machine guns.

Hazel in her Chinese
wadded garment.

# CHAPTER 9

## MISSION INTERRUPTED

The Chinese were suffering horrible abuse—electric shocks, hangings and shootings. The missionaries in the clinic treated gunshot wounds without asking questions. John Kuhn spent each night in the clinic to prevent the military from using the mission buildings as billets. Hazel and Jean Kirkpatrick alternated spending the nights there, too, so extra space at both the clinic and the Mission home was filled. In June, soldiers came from the capital and the situation eased. In August, Hazel received a Christmas parcel from home. It had been only ten months on the way!

Hazel was preparing to attend Edith's wedding in Kunming, when a telegram arrived. Language students from around the world would be arriving shortly in Chungking, but the teachers were stranded in Shanghai. Could Hazel come to Chungking and help? Hazel sorted through every trunk to find the things she would need for winter wear. The only transportation available for the eight-day trip from Paoshan to Kunming was on top of a truckload of baled cotton. So she and her baggage started out. A big straw hat tied on with a kerchief protected her from the sun, but when it poured rain, even that didn't help. She arrived in Kunming the day after Edith Broadfoot married Dr. John Toop. (They would continue to work at the Paoshan Hospital.) Since she wasn't in time to be the maid of honour as planned, Hazel visited them at their honeymoon cottage. Ever after they joked about Hazel joining them on their honeymoon!

She was thankful to go the rest of the way by plane, from Kunming to Chungking. It was so difficult to get funds that smaller missions were withdrawing their missionaries and the plane was loaded. There was no promise that all her luggage would make it, so friends suggested that Hazel wear as much as she could. She boarded the plane wearing five dresses and four extra blouses. It was fine in Kunming, where it was not too hot, Hazel admitted, but when they arrived in Chungking and had to walk up the hill to the house, she was very hot. Language students began arriving at the Chungking Theological Seminary from Australia, England, the United States, Germany and South Africa.

By November the Communists were coming towards Chungking, too. For only the second time in her life, Hazel had a battle with fear. The Communists hadn't moved into the Paoshan area. Would she be able to get back there? The Lutheran mission plane, the *St. Paul*, would first have to come into Chungking and take her to Hong Kong, but would it even be allowed to land? If not, then what?

Edna McLaren, from New Zealand, usually joined Hazel for prayer each evening. One night, realising that Hazel was not at peace about her future, Edna lovingly suggested that maybe Hazel was not trusting God to do the best for her. Into Hazel's mind popped the memory of dealing with this same type of fear in candidate school. Quickly she asked forgiveness for not trusting the Lord and committed all of her fears to Him. The next morning the St. Paul arrived.

Hazel breathed a sigh of relief as she settled into her seat in the plane. But they weren't in the air yet. Bullets whizzed past the window of the plane as the Lord again proved His faithfulness and lifted them safely into the air. In Hong Kong she wrote letters while she waited to return to her work. On December 5 she flew back into China.

Kunming City was peacefully turned over to the Liberators, as the Communists called themselves, while she was there. Now she just had to find a way back home to

Paoshan. It could only have been the Lord who sent a Christian Chinese lady, Mrs. Wang, and her four-year-old son, to escort Hazel part of the way. Mrs. Wang instructed Hazel not to say a word in Chinese or even let on she understood it. Even her facial expressions must be guarded. For three days they travelled, waited while bridges were mended, took detours, slept in the truck, and stopped at various places to register, or for examination. Once, when the truck was detained, Hazel and Mrs. Wang walked over an hour to an inn, praying the truck would be allowed to pass in the morning. A carrier handled their baggage, which was heavy with silver coins. When Hazel and Mrs. Wang arrived at Hsiakuan, they were amazed to find John Kuhn (who had taken twenty days to get there), and Larry Peet, also waiting for a truck. The next day they all left for Paoshan, and it was a comfort to Hazel to travel with other missionaries.

The Mekong River presented another delay. The truck needed repairs and the bridge was dangerously weak. They proceeded to unload the truck and carry everything over the bridge so the truck could cross over empty. Then the truck was repaired. When that was done, everything was reloaded. It had taken all day just to cross the river and it was too late to go on. That night, Christmas Eve, they sat around a charcoal fire in a little food shop and sang Christmas carols. Attracted by their singing, local people drifted in. John Kuhn read the Christmas story and explained the extent of Jesus' love for them. Then the missionaries passed around oranges and candy.

Trees were in flower as they set out Christmas morning for Paoshan. They arrived safely before dark and then heard the other side of the story. An armed robber had known the route these foreigners were taking. While their truck stopped for the night, another truck from Hsiakuan went ahead. During the afternoon, along a lonely stretch of road, that truck was robbed of money, valuables, and even coats.

Christians from the three main outstations were in Paoshan, and the reunion was pleasant but brief. The CIM still had a lot of work to do in China, but how much time did they have left? Now that Edith was married, Hazel was assigned to work with Anna Pfautz again, but this time in Lungling, where Anna was already working with Victor and Leita Christianson.

The road going that direction was not open for trucks, so Mr. Kuhn arranged for Larry Peet to escort Hazel the four-and-a-half-days' walk with packhorses. Hazel had known Larry Peet from candidate school in Philadelphia. She remembered him at school, standing on his balcony in the morning, singing them all awake with his wonderful voice, "Good morning friends, it's time to rise and start the day." With her things collected from Paoshan, it took eleven horses to move her to Lungling. Her sewing machine was almost one load. She also had about fifty pounds of tracts, posters and calendars to use in the work and about as much in flannelgraph materials and Bibles. Each horse carried one hundred sixty pounds.

As they wound their way high among the pines, Hazel saw Shan people in the distance, unique with their high turbans, long full skirts, tight leggings and silver buttons on their blouses. These were the people she and Anna would eventually be working with. Looking down through the breaks in the trees, she could also see the Salween River, like a green snake winding through the mountain valley.

The orderly loading and unloading of the horses was an amazing sight. Every animal had a packsaddle of padded wood, which went on first. Two men then lifted each load up onto the packsaddle and fastened it. Whenever they stopped for a meal, the horsemen worked together to lift off the loads, take off the packsaddles, and let the horses go loose in the fields. When it was time to go, each horse came promptly to his owner when called, and the routine was reversed. In ten minutes the caravan was on its way again. Day after day of hiking was taking its toll on Hazel's feet, and within weeks she would lose several toenails. She had no choice but to press on. The days were long, but the nights were short. They slept out under the stars at night, just a few feet from the horses' hooves, until breakfast was called at 2:30 in the morning. Hazel was relieved to arrive at her destination.

Lungling was very close to Burma. Preparations for an upcoming conference were already underway. As people from surrounding areas began arriving, it became evident that many were suffering from infected teeth. Hazel already had experience in pulling a tooth and hated to see these people suffering. Using pliers, she pulled seven or eight teeth and packed each cavity with cotton soaked in hydrogen peroxide. It was a case of using what she had and the patients were all fine.

Going to the market for groceries was always interesting, but now it became a burden, in a real way. The coins they used had holes in the centre and were strung on heavy cords. A knot was tied between each hundred coins. Big silver coins were worth about twelve cents Canadian. Twenty-cent coins were about the size of a nickel. For anything smaller they used copper coins, and seven hundred copper coins made up fifty cents in silver. Now the weight of the money she needed to go to market was almost more than the weight of what she bought and carried home.

As part of her continuing language studies, Hazel's next assignment was to translate the first twenty chapters of Exodus, the first eight chapters of Leviticus, Judges, Ruth and I Samuel, from English to Chinese, before writing her next examination. Hazel often studied with her plastic tablecloth overhead on the rafters to catch the termite dust. Termites and mould were two more things they had to contend with. Hazel wore different shoes each day just to keep them from moulding. Then there were preparations for Sunday school, when 160 children came to learn about the Lord.

Hazel's letters to family and friends were always a work in progress. She would add to them continually, so that if someone was going out with mail, at a moment's notice she simply finished the letters and sent them off, sometimes to be mailed from Burma, sometimes from other places in China.

All through her missionary career, her letters spanned weeks, sometimes even months.

The plan now was for Hazel and Anna to move down onto the plain to work with the Shan people. Mrs. Pretel, an associate missionary, worked about twenty miles from Lungling, only a few miles from the border of Burma. Hazel and Anna made several trips into this needy area to hand out literature. Then, one day, Communist soldiers stopped them, seized all their tracts and ripped them up. The girls were told never to come back.

The presence of foreigners was making things increasingly more dangerous for the native believers. Finally a directive was issued from headquarters: "It is with sorrow of heart that we have reached the conclusion that we must proceed with a planned withdrawal of our missionaries." It had been eighty-five years since the CIM began working in China. The telegram reached Lungling on January 3, 1951, almost six years to the day since Hazel had arrived in China.

Hazel began to sort her things and sell what she could. She sent four parcels of books and seven envelopes and other parcels home to Canada. She was concerned about sending her stamp collection home. Then she came up with a plan. Cutting the centre out of every third page of a hard cover book, she arranged a layer of stamps in this cut out area and glued the edges of the three pages together. This book full of stamps, still retaining the thickness of the original book, was mailed, and arrived safely in Victoria.

Hazel, Anna and the Christiansons left Lungling and made their way to Paoshan. While they waited there for their passes, Hazel made dresses out of all the material she had. "There may be a question about carrying material," she thought, "but dresses shouldn't matter." She also took pity on Mr. Kuhn. He had been robbed and everything he had was in tatters. He was desperately in need of a dress shirt. Hazel found several new white sheets left behind by other missionaries. Using one of his old shirts as a pattern, she made several white dress shirts and some shorts for him. His wife and son had already been safely evacuated via Burma.

"I have mailed all my snaps but one or two and also some of my diplomas. I guess I'd better burn my diary," she wrote in one letter home. Another short note from Paoshan stated, "I'm just sending the pages out of my notebook so it will save time on the road. They would have to be searched each time we stopped. This afternoon I looked through some trunks of stuff belonging to others." The missionaries were asked to go through these things to make sure nothing was left behind that would incriminate the Mission, or anything that would be considered a weapon. Hopefully people reading her notes would go to their knees to pray.

They did find weapons—a shotgun and a pistol. How could they dispose of these without the Communist military finding out? They were puzzling over this when the mission watchdog died. Wrapping up the dead dog, the missionaries boldly carried this burden through the streets in Chinese fashion and dropped it into the river, weighed down with rocks. And weapons!

"We are learning these days to place less value on the things of this world which pass away," Hazel wrote on March 12. Everything they had left behind in Lungling was taken over by the government. The money they received from the sale of their belongings was confiscated. Her precious Handy Andy, hidden under the steps, would never be retrieved. Hazel now took with her a small trunk, two suitcases and a bed roll, all that was left of the eleven loads carried up there on pack horses.

They bade a sorrowful farewell to their Chinese friends, praying that they would be safe. "We got off from Paoshan on March 23 and were given nine days to reach Kunming." Charcoal-powered trucks normally didn't have enough power to make it up the steep hills as they went from Paoshan in the Mekong valley, over the Tali mountain range. They would drive until the engine stalled. Then they would quickly shove a wedge behind the front wheel, while they restarted the engine and continued on until it stalled again. The truck Hazel was on used a bit of gasoline on the hills, so it did better than the others, and had only one breakdown. Each morning everything had to be loaded and rearranged.

"We are a big crowd in Kunming now. I am with thirty others in one mission house. There are twenty-four at the other mission house. When the rest from Mitu and Tali come there will be over seventy. Some may have left by then too." Mrs. Pretel wanted desperately to get a hymnbook in the Tai language printed before she left and Hazel was pleased to help leave literature behind. She was back in the printing business. Ironic that she would be used to help leave behind a hymnbook again! The songs were full of doctrine!

Whenever the Communist officials felt like it, they hauled the missionaries in to fill out paperwork. Except for a few words, it was all in Chinese characters. After a couple of trips, Hazel realised that she was filling out the same document each time. Secretly, she wrote down the details they asked for so her answers would always be the same. In total she filled out seven documents (four papers to a set). April plodded by with no passes, then May. It became obvious that they were being detained until their funds were exhausted. Finally, on the last day of May they had permission to go as soon as seats were available on a plane. That didn't happen. They had been living in crowded conditions long enough, so the missionaries made their own arrangements—by truck to Chungking, by boat to Hankow, then by train to the border.

Hazel wrote about the evacuation:

"We were late setting out because it took so long to have all our baggage inspected. They opened every towel, felt every shoulder pad and pocket and any other thick places on any garment. I had my bedding sewn inside a sheet and bedspread to keep it clean but the girls who examined my things undid all the sewing and pulled things apart." Hazel was being polite, not wanting her family to worry. The inspectors were not kind. They took out the potholders and matching case that Aunt Sadie had given to Florence (black sateen cloth with butterflies embroidered on them), and decided it was ancient Chinese embroidery. She couldn't take that! (Aunt Sadie's embroidery was so well done, no wonder they claimed it as their own.) Hazel had her Chinese shoes on inside her runners and they went unnoticed.

In her trunk was the kettle her mother had sent to China with her. Lifting the lid, the inspector saw Hazel's collection of small toys, including carved wooden sheep covered with flannel, a porcelain whistle, and other small toys that had belonged to her father. When asked what they were, Hazel replied, "These were my Honourable Father's toys and are cherished." The elderly are highly revered by the Chinese. The inspector put the toys back and closed the lid. Hazel breathed a sigh of relief. Layered inside the kettle were photographs of Chinese friends, silver spoons and Chinese coins. The group was often stopped and examined—always their possessions and sometimes even a body search. At the Hankow border it was raining. The inspectors there were especially rough and nasty.

Only one train a day went from Canton to the border, so they had to wait for it. Finally, on July 11, 1951, after months of waiting, preparing and travel, they arrived in Hong Kong.

# CHAPTER 10

## A NEW FOCUS

It is hard to imagine what was going on behind the scene, with all of the missionaries landing in Hong Kong with no place to go and very few belongings. In a series of miracles, eleven Quonset huts were obtained to house them. The logistics of making travel arrangements for so many to return to their various homes is almost incomprehensible. Hazel was faced with a decision. Where should she go? Home to Canada? The Mission had informed everyone that they would receive funds for another four months.

One option Hazel had was to apply to work with Wycliffe Bible Translators again. She wrote to them about that possibility before she even left China. A letter from Ken Pike of Wycliffe Bible Translators reached her, and his reply was not what she expected. "You obviously did not know at the time of your writing that the plans of the CIM had been altered considerably and that they are now ready to expand into … points where there are Chinese-speaking peoples." Two places he mentioned interested Hazel: Thailand and the Philippines. She immediately informed the Mission.

A wonderful surprise awaited Hazel, though, before she even left Hong Kong. Unbeknownst to her, the *HMCS Sioux*, a naval ship doing a tour of duty in that part of the world, slid into the Hong Kong harbour for repairs. Hazel was stunned to receive a phone call from her brother John. He was there! In Hong Kong! One of the ship's crew, John was scheduled to go into the hospital to get treatment for a rash. First he wanted to see his sister. Hazel remembered John as a very affectionate brother, and he didn't disappoint her. When his taxi arrived at the CIM office, the siblings greeted each other with hugs and tears. They chatted over tea for a long time and then went to a restaurant, had ice cream sodas and talked some more. Hazel visited him at the hospital during the week. "We talked about old days at home, how Saskatoon has grown, about his car, his leather work, about China and my work there." What a miracle that they would be in Hong Kong at the same time, but for such different reasons.

To sail directly to North America meant Hazel would have to disembark in San Francisco and possibly be stranded in the USA for months. The United States Government had orders not to issue visas for anyone coming from Communist China for two to four months. Hazel would rather spend the time seeing more of the world, so on August 2 she left Hong Kong, with other missionaries, bound for England.

See the world, she did! They sailed to Aden on the south tip of Saudi Arabia, then through the Suez Canal, where small boats came alongside the ship to sell curios. Hazel bought a bone brooch with little dangling elephants. At Port Said they went ashore on a pontoon bridge, another first for Hazel. At Ceuta, Spanish Morocco, they were reminded of the local dress codes before they left the ship. Finally, after a month at sea, they arrived in London.

"We have been distressed at the attempts of reporters and others to get information privately from our workers coming from China," a letter of warning from the Mission stated. "If anyone should approach you, please make no statement but refer them to the headquarters of the mission." The missionaries were also advised that "no communication of any kind (written or printed) should be sent to national Christians in China. The simplest kind of news may be misconstrued and do harm to the recipient." What a disappointment to Hazel, who loved to write letters. She prayed that Christian radio broadcasts would soon be able to reach her Chinese friends.

Hazel had several weeks to rethink her future, because the earliest she could expect to leave for Canada was September 29. What did the Lord have planned for her future? It looked like this was the end of her ministry in China, but was it the end of her missionary work entirely? She had been obedient to the Lord's call to China. Now she was ready to serve the Lord anywhere! Before she left England, a letter arrived from Herbert Griffin of CIM. "I appreciate your putting yourself in the hands of our Mission leaders concerning the field. Mr. Pittman of Wycliffe was glad to learn that you are considering the Philippines ... How soon could you be ready?" Just that quickly Hazel's future was decided.

With a light heart she joined other missionaries to tour Regent's Park Zoo, ride a tram, and visit Madame Tussaud's Wax Works, London Tower and Windsor Castle. A physical exam indicated she was in good health. She got her passport, vaccination and inoculations. In many respects the boat trip back to Canada was a repeat of the trip out. Many were seasick. Hazel looked after a baby part of each afternoon, since both parents were sick. The ship was Italian and the steward's language much like Spanish. Hazel took the opportunity to brush up on her Spanish.

Hazel stepped onto Canadian soil at Halifax on October 6, 1951, three months after she had left China. Tickets were waiting for her at the Canadian National Railroad office. With a new ministry in her future, she sent most of her luggage home, while she set off across Canada and the United States to raise prayer support for her future work in the Philippines. She visited Irvine and Vi and their families. In Saskatoon she took a stroll past her former home, recalling past memories she had so recently shared with her brother John.

It was an exciting evening when she finally arrived home and opened her boxes and trunks. Everything evoked an exciting story to tell her parents, especially the kettle! Even as she unpacked, she was thinking about what she would need for the Philippines. This time she would pack dental tools. She was determined that if she ever pulled another tooth she would not be restricted to a pair of pliers. It would be over a year, though, before everything was in place and she could be on her way again.

The waves were gigantic, tossing the ship around on the ocean. Hazel loved it! She was celebrating her thirty-sixth birthday on board a Danish freighter headed for a new ministry in the Philippines. The storm was the Lord's birthday present to her. That was also the day they crossed the International Date Line. That would be fine, she stated, to miss the day and stay a year younger. It was 1953 and Hazel had already been corresponding with her new partner in the Philippines. Frances Williamson was working with the Iraya people. While she sailed, Hazel studied the next language she would be learning. Hazel liked Frances as soon as she met her.

Manila reminded her of Mexico: stop lights at some corners, police with whistles and signs at others, and buses and jeepneys. But these buses and jeepneys were built for short people. Hazel learned to sit by the aisle, where her knees could protrude and folks could edge by. She would never forget her surprise when the conductor put his hand up to his ear to get twenty cents change for her. For convenience, they put the coins in their ears. A convenience not yet discovered in Canada, she quipped.

The Pittmans, missionaries from Mexico, were now working in Manila, and Hazel was pleased to meet them again. She toured the Far Eastern Bible Institute and Seminary. Hazel was intrigued with the amazing little radio sets that Mr. Blake made at The Far East Broadcasting Company (FEBC). Pre-tuned to Christian stations, they were sent into remote areas so that the tribal people could hear the Word of God every day in the trade language.

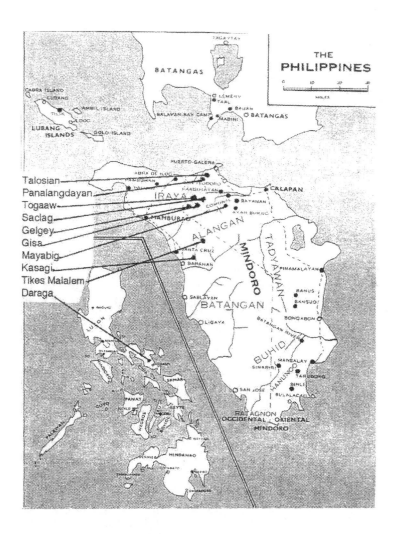

Manila is on the Island of Luzon, one of seven thousand Philippine Islands. But Luzon was not Hazel's final destination. Loaded down with eleven pieces of baggage, Frances and Hazel travelled by bus to Batangas, on the southwest coast, where they boarded a boat. Their destination was Mindoro, the seventh largest of the Philippine Islands. Hazel found Mindoro lush with jungle and coconut palms. The larger towns and cities were located along the coast, while mountains rising 8,000 feet covered the

75

inland portion of the island. Over the years, as more and more people had arrived from other islands and took their land, the tribal people had run away, moving further up the mountains where they cultivated the land. These were the people the Mission wanted to reach.

In Calapan, the capital of Oriental (eastern) Mindoro, they purchased a bed for Hazel, a desk, a cupboard for the phonograph, a screen cupboard for food, a bench for visitors and two stools for themselves. All of this amounted to only $45! A little extra paid to have it all bused twenty or so miles to San Teodoro, where they would set up their home base. They bought fruits, vegetables and bread and headed home.

Several things about her new home surprised Hazel. It was on stilts. The windows had no screen or glass, only sliding shutters, and the roof was made of nipa palm fronds. It didn't take long to arrange everything in the 12' X 13' house. A table and three chairs filled the dining area, and both of their stoves sat on a large box at the kitchen end of the room. The other half of the house, divided by a curtain, was their sleeping quarters. Hazel realised that the entire house was the size of her parents' living room! There was no living room here unless you considered the other table and bench on the porch. Another surprise awaited her. The little "out-house", built over the lagoon, flushed whenever the tide came in.

Once they were settled into this home base, it was time to begin visiting the tribal areas. There were six distinct tribes and language groups on the island, and the girls would be working with the Iraya people in Oriental Mindoro. The other side of the island was Occidental (western) Mindoro.

Hazel would never forget her first trip out to their tribal destination. It was raining and a new road was being built part way up the mountain. They slipped and slogged through the sticky wet soil. Was this really the right way? Or had Frances taken her off the beaten track to test her? After crossing the river, which came well up over Hazel's knees, they travelled a rutted water buffalo trail. Leeches were numerous, but they were not like any leeches Hazel had encountered in Canada. Thin and string-like, they could make their way through looser weaves of clothing. "Keep pulling them off," Frances advised her. Once attached, they inject an anti-coagulant, making the blood flow freely when they are pulled off. Easier said than done, on a trek like this.

Kaagutayan was a beautiful spot in the jungle. Just above a small river, the village looked out on mountains on all sides. Hazel basked in the spectacular view. The house, made of poles, with palm walls and roof, was almost invisible in the midst of the jungle foliage. A new 9' X 12' room just added to the former 9' X 12' area was designated as their bedroom. Hazel's odd looking Fuller shower was hung in a corner behind a curtain. This was a galvanised pail, flat on one side, with a tap and a hose with a brush attached. When it was filled with water, they only had to turn the tap, aim the hose and—presto!—a shower. Excess water ran through the split bamboo slats of the floor.

The people were Hazel's main interest. Small compared to her, with straight black hair, sparkling dark eyes and swarthy skin, they shyly approached, men wearing only G-strings and women wearing not much else. Hazel and Frances, with their modest clothes, were the ones who were out of place here. Hazel would get used to it. This was now her second home. These people were now her family.

Frances arranged for them to hold Bible classes at the Mangyan (a term referring to all tribal people) residential school at Saclag, a village between Kaagutayan and San Teodoro. The first time they went there, Hazel taught the children Genesis 1:1 (In the beginning, God created the heaven and the earth), from the Tagalog Bible and also in English. Then Frances told the story in Tagalog and asked questions in English. Neither of them had ever used Tagalog in a meeting before. Their ministry was off and running! And Hazel discovered the muddy route they came on was the main road!

Hazel was never without pencil and paper. She would hear a word and write it down phonetically. By the end of March she had over one thousand words recorded in Tagalog and Iraya and began to make an English/Tagalog/Iraya file, like a dictionary. Learning the Tagalog language was the missionaries' main priority, so they studied Friday afternoon, Saturday morning and Monday morning at San Teodoro before going to the village. Monday to Friday they were in Kaagutayan and taught at the Saclag School each Friday on their way back to San Teodoro. It was important to move continually from place to place. If they left one place for any length of time, they would return to find shoes and suitcases mouldy. Their goal was to eventually learn the Iraya language, but they also wanted to master Tagalog, the trade language of Mindoro.

Hazel quickly fell in love with the Iraya people. She was thrilled to be in Kaagutayan one day when the Governor of Oriental Mindoro came to visit. Up until now, the only government official who had ever visited this little village was the mayor of San Teodoro. This day, people came from all the outlying areas and happily listened to gospel records while they waited for the Governor to arrive. Even the mayor listened to one record. The Governor came, visited and left. It was exciting, but not nearly as exciting as what followed.

Anghel Anias, the leader of this little village and first Mangyan Christian convert, gathered everyone around the missionaries' porch. Using their picture of Jesus on the cross, he explained that Jesus had died for them, had been raised from the dead and was coming back again. The girls were thankful to know that the village leader himself was a bold believer. Anghel was willing to answer their curious questions. Hazel had a question for him.

"I hear people singing in the night. What are they singing about?"

Anghel explained. It was an old Mangyan custom from the days of their forefathers. When anyone was sick, they would sacrifice a pig and sing to the spirits. "But now we have told them about God's Son, Jesus, dying for them", he quickly added, "and they know there is a better way." Many of his people still needed to hear about Jesus. These women were here to tell that story, and he was here to help them.

"We are trying out our new alphabet with five vowels and fifteen consonants. So far it seems satisfactory," Hazel wrote home. Their day usually began around 5:00 A.M. and at 7:30 A.M. they had a class with Anghel. The days were long, but there were little bits of entertainment to alleviate their hard work. They had a lizard, a Tuko, living in the roof. It was aptly named, because every once in a while it called out loudly, "Too koo, too koo." Hazel rather enjoyed having wildlife around, as long as it didn't bite.

The Mission needed a name change now that they were not working in China. Mr. Griffin (the North American Home Director), Dr. Canfield (Assistant Director in Singapore), and Marie Barham, who worked with the Buhid tribe, arrived to visit at the end of May. These visitors represented the new China Inland Mission Overseas Missionary Fellowship. On the mission field they would use only Overseas Missionary Fellowship or OMF. Hazel wondered how they would manage the trip to Kaagutayan, but they had a good trip up. The group had lunch there, then Anghel helped demonstrate their language study. They stopped at the school at Saclag as well and visited with the principal. The trip back out was not easy. It had rained and the men were wearing leather oxfords, but they took it in stride.

The three-day mission conference in Manila followed their visit. Hazel loved conferences. She could stay with Cyril and Doris Weller, now working in the Philippines, too. They were, and always would be, Hazel's family on the mission field. Hazel was pleased to learn that People's Church in Toronto had again taken up her support.

Hazel recorded a word that meant, "to carry something." Then she learned another word that meant, "to carry on the head." A slightly different word meant, "to carry on shoulders"; another was used "to carry it dangling from the hand." What started out as one word had grown into many. How could she remember them all? Hazel was determined to learn the language quickly, because she found it very hard to speak by "interruption", as someone called it.

Hazel sitting on the steps of her house.

# CHAPTER 11

## MAYABIG

Language! There is no way most people can really understand God's Word unless they read it in their own language. In Mindoro several tribal groups, including the Iraya, did not have the Word in their own tongue; they didn't even have their language written down. There was a lot of work to be done, but where to start? Someone first has to record enough of the language to figure out an alphabet. Being an avid student of languages and with that keen ear, Hazel could do that. Marie Barham's visit was no accident. She had worked in China, too, and also had Wycliffe training, but she needed help with the Buhid language in the south part of Mindoro. Hazel, with her God-given ability to mimic and to write down phonetically what she heard, was asked to help Marie. If native speakers would help a few hours a day for several days, they could work out an alphabet.

They visited three different areas to check the sounds. This was not going to be easy. They had discovered three different dialects. Before they could translate the Scriptures into the Buhid language, they needed to know if the dialects overlapped and if the people of the three areas understood one another. Hazel returned to the Iraya people and left Marie with a lot of research to do.

The Mission was still in the process of registering in the Philippines, so all the missionaries held only four-month visitor's visas. In August, Hazel had to make the long trip back to Manila to sign the papers for another four months. It

81

was an expense for the missionaries, and it took a lot of travel time! Hazel quickly learned to make every trip to Manila a multiple-task trip. Before she left the tribal area in August, Hazel translated a short story and tried it out on several people who could read. "When the Bee Stung Mother" was a story the Iraya people could understand. A little boy's mother protected him from a bee, and was stung herself. Then his mother used it as an illustration of how Jesus took our punishment and died for our sins. While Hazel was in Manila, she cut a stencil and ran off copies on the copier. She was also preparing simple reading lessons for the people.

Rice harvest had a double meaning to Hazel as she watched the people labour together. First they cut off of the rice heads by hand. "They carry them to a threshing floor, tread them out with their feet, winnow them and then pound the kernels in a mortar to get the husks off. When we realise the amount of work they put into this visible harvest, which soon will be consumed, we are reminded that it is not going to be an easy task for us to bring in a harvest of souls in the Mangyan area. Prayer is harder work than preaching but both are essential." Hazel's letters were filled with stories like that, top to bottom. She thought it was a waste of a good stamp if you didn't write in all the space, so her margins were very scanty and sometimes the last line was written vertically up the side. Often she had a little sketch or a small bug taped in the corner of the page. She had a scale to weigh outgoing letters, and if weight allowed, she'd add another page.

Hazel and Frances worked on translating the story of the Lost Sheep, so that Frances could take it to Manila with her when she went on vacation. It was a story requested by Anghel. When Frances returned with the printed story at the end of November, she also brought the good news that their immigration papers for the next five years were ready. Then she added even better news. They didn't have to go to Manila. They could put signature or thumbprint on the papers in Calapan. They were in Mindoro to stay!

Life in the tribal area became almost routine, back and forth from San Teodoro to Kaagutayan each week, language study, teaching, translation. But then, once in a while, something unusual would suddenly change the picture. One night the river flooded. By the time Hazel and Frances were on the way back to San Teodoro the next day, the water had receded so they began to wade across as usual. Suddenly Frances lost her footing. Unable to swim, she was in danger of being quickly swept down the river. Hazel lunged after her, grabbed Frances and managed to keep her afloat. Shoulder deep in swiftly moving water, they struggled to save their belongings as well as themselves. When they finally made it to the shore the bank was a steep, difficult climb. Hazel had her pack suspended from a band around her forehead. Now as she boosted Frances up out of the water, her pack slipped off and floated away. After making sure Frances was safe, Hazel turned to swim after her belongings.

"Don't! Crocodiles!" Frances shouted. Hazel stopped short. They had drifted near a deep part of the river where a tribal man had been attacked by crocodiles and had lost his leg. Sadly Hazel watched her bag float away. In it were her flannelgraph materials, a hand-written book of Tagalog stories, a hand-written book of Mangyan stories and her Boy Scout knife. Although Frances had copies of all the language materials, Hazel now had to re-copy them into new notebooks, a long job! Hazel's watch, a keepsake that had belonged to her sister Florence, was soaked. Thankfully, when it dried it worked again.

Hazel's first Christmas in the Philippines, 1953, was made especially enjoyable by a visit from her friend Sunny Beth, now working in the Philippines with Child Evangelism. Hazel, Sunny Beth and Frances handed out Christmas tracts to almost every home in San Teodoro. Then they went to Calapan for the annual year-end Day of Prayer. Seven new missionaries had increased the number of adult OMF workers in Mindoro to twelve. When Sunny Beth returned to her own work, Margrit Furrer (another OMF'er from China) arrived in San Teodoro to study Tagalog.

It was impossible for Hazel and Frances to be at all the villages all the time, so technically, the "Portable Missionary", a little radio set made by Mr. Blake, was the "resident missionary" in Kaagutayan and many other places. Pre-tuned to DZAS, the Christian station operated by Far East Broadcasting, the radio was kept at Anghel's house. Up to twenty-five people would come in the evening to listen to the half-hour program in Tagalog, and if the girls were not there, Anghel would lead the people in singing and worship.

It seemed like a bonanza when Joy Hayman from Australia and Caroline Stickley from the USA arrived to help in the work early in 1954. They paired up. Frances and Caroline stayed in San Teodoro for a week while Joy and Hazel went to Kaagutayan. The next week they changed places. Then Caroline and Joy settled down to study and minister in San Teodoro, and that freed Hazel and Frances to branch out into new places. One of these places was a village of seventeen houses along the Mayabig River. Ten minutes from there, at Bayanan, was a government school. It was similar to the situation at Kaagutayan and Saclag.

Previously, a Christian teacher in Bayanan had died with malignant malaria. She had a missionary heart, and before she died she told the people about Jesus. They all missed her and were also hungry for more teaching from the Word. Even though it took an hour by bus and another hour and a half of walking, crossing rivers and streams, to reach the village, every new outreach was an answer to prayer.

Schooling was a constant problem for the tribal people. The school at Saclag was a residential school, but the one at Bayanan wasn't, so children coming from a distance had to live with relatives. Parents in the outlying areas were in constant conflict about having to send their children away to school. In April a meeting was arranged at Saclag to address the problem, with tribal people from the surrounding mountainous regions. The missionaries were there, too, to make contact. The school issue had made the people wary. There was only one thing to do. "We'll visit them!"

When the people at Kaagutayan heard that these single missionary women were contemplating a trip even farther into the mountains, they said, "Oh, it's very far. The road is hard. There are many leeches, big ones, squirming everywhere along the way. You must take soap to rub on your legs and arms; then the leeches will not be able to fasten on to your flesh and draw your blood."

"Are there many people?" the girls asked. "There are many," was the reply. That was all the incentive these missionaries needed. The fact that there were lots of people waiting to hear the Gospel was enough to urge Hazel and Caroline onto the trail. Hazel was eager to know how many people spoke only Iraya and to determine if extensive translation was really needed. Most of the people understood Tagalog, but how much did they comprehend? Records arrived from Gospel Recordings, just in time, with messages both in Tagalog and Iraya, the local language. They would be a great help in reaching these timid people who had never heard the good news of salvation in their own tongue. Toring and Rudolpo, teen-aged boys, agreed to guide Hazel and Caroline on this trip. They set off, carrying bedding, mosquito nets, food, and most importantly, phonograph and records.

The people were right. Hungry leeches were everywhere, sometimes as many as ten at a time clinging to one wound on their skin. The trail was muddy, but the boys helped the women in dangerous spots, cut branches that were in the way, and removed leeches from their shoes. Toring jumped and ran up and down the mountains with an amazing amount of energy. Soon the girls were calling him "Bouncy". Rudolpo let out a war whoop every so often, so that earned him the nickname "Whoopsie".

Their first stop was Binaybay, where quite a few people listened to the records. Their next stop was Toring's home, a village of only two houses. Here Hazel read the story of the Lost Sheep and bound up some sores. Moving on, they followed the river about twenty minutes and then for forty-five minutes climbed over rocky trails and logs to arrive at Ayan Itum. Rudolpo had gradually taken charge of the phonograph and now took great pride in playing all the records. It had been a long day, so they decided to stay overnight here. Hazel was ready for a good night's rest. It wasn't to be. The place was alive with wild forest roaches (cockroaches less than a half-inch long) crawling and biting. Added to that, a huge hog was penned under the porch where the girls were sleeping. All night he grunted and pushed his snout up between the poles of the floor at regular intervals, sending the girls into smothered giggles. Most of the night the missionaries just wished for morning. At daylight they removed at least a hundred roaches from their belongings as they packed. Meanwhile, Toring had disappeared. He was away with a purpose. He returned with several men in tow to hear all the records before they left.

After a short hike downhill to the Laylay River, they started to climb once more. It was a hard, steep climb. Across the valley they could see the village they had just left. Soon they could see the ocean and even Calapan far in the distance. At another village of two houses, Rudolpo cooked the rice they had brought with them. Strangely, no one else in the house was cooking. Hazel asked why and discovered that the family had no food. What had been planned for the four travellers was shared with a family of six. But the spiritual food they shared with these long-sought-after people was most important. After the scanty meal they began the return trip and stopped at each of the homes they had visited on the way up. A bit of candy they found in their gear helped quiet their growling stomachs.

The people at Mayabig River wanted Hazel to live there and teach them. Hazel was willing, but first they would need to supply a house for her. The folks at Bayanan School claimed they already had a house ready for her. It needed a little repair, they reported, but she could move in that afternoon. Hazel wasn't prepared to move quite that fast, but the following week she did move to Bayanan. The 6' X 8' thatched roof house on stilts had not been prepared at all. She scrubbed the slat floor, set up a shelf for her stove and put up nails to hang things on. This house was not built for someone five feet, eight inches tall. The walls came up to her shoulders, and when she stood up, her head was well up into the roof part. She could see out over the walls only by sitting down on her one box. The villagers did keep her well supplied with food in exchange for medicine.

People gathered and sat patiently watching her get settled. They were waiting to hear the records. The Lord had obviously prepared the way. Hearts were hungry for the message of salvation. Several adults came, their black hair shining, their bare brown limbs sleek and slim, wanting to be sure their sins were forgiven. They asked Christ to take away their sins and then went away to tell others. Even Tagalog people, who came to sell things or to hire field help, heard the good news, and some professed to trust the Lord. Some days the records were played eight to ten hours.

Hazel called on her past experience from the reading campaign in Mexico and developed primers to teach adults to read. She used very simple Tagalog for the Iraya believers in Bayanan who spoke Tagalog most of the time. Then she spent hours copying the twenty-page primer, using her hand duplicator. The Bible was available in Tagalog, so people who had never learned to read would soon be able to read the Word themselves. Things were going great.

"Let's kill her! We'll see if there is a God. I don't believe there is a God! Let's kill her." Hazel was awakened from a sound sleep by men returning to the village, shouting and boisterous. Women were not left alone at night, so usually one or two children slept at her house. This night the children couldn't be with her, so Hazel was alone. She understood immediately what the men's intentions were. Silently, she sat up in the dark on her sleeping mat.

Hazel's house was virtually wall-less, no protection at all. She could see nothing in the dark, but God could. She began to pray. The men came to where they would turn into her lane. Suddenly there was an eerie silence. Hazel sat still, scarcely breathing. A little later she heard low, excited conversations in the village, then silence again.

"Were you afraid last night?" An early morning visitor asked the next day. Hazel told the truth. Yes, but when she prayed, the fear left. Then she heard the rest of the story. A man, who often came home drunk, was full of bravado as he yelled, "We'll see if there is a God!" He decided to kill Hazel. When the man haughtily approached the entrance to her lane, he stopped suddenly. Terrified, he silenced the other men and rushed home.

"I was coming to kill you," the man himself told Hazel later. "But on each side of your lane, there was a guard dressed in white. I was afraid to try to pass them." The Lord had sent His protecting angels. Hazel's mother had been prompted to pray for Hazel at that exact time and had prayed until she knew that Hazel's need had been met. Another friend had also been urged to pray for her at the very time she was in danger. Hazel wrote in her diary, "How wonderful to learn that at the very hour of my need God found at least two at home who were sensitive to His voice and upheld me in prayer." It wasn't long before the man who had wanted to kill her gave his own life to the Lord.

One night in Bayanan Hazel was startled when a woman came running, breathless, to her house. "People heard noises on the path and were frightened," she gasped. They were not human sounds, they said, but some sort of plague or evil spirit. Should they run to the mountains? These people had a continual battle with fear of the unknown. A bit of prying revealed that the last time this had happened was just before Pearl Harbour was bombed. No wonder they were so frightened. But now those who believed in Jesus had another way to deal with fear. Soon more than thirty people filled Hazel's new larger house, some carrying their bundles, prepared to flee. Hazel read the Word to them. She reminded them of God's power and prayed for peace for them. Six people prayed that night, confessing sin and claiming God's forgiveness. Not one ran to the mountains, and everyone had a good sleep.

The Alangan, another tribe of people, bordered close to Bayanan, but were mostly in Occidental Mindoro. They too needed Gospel records in their language. Hazel was given the job of gathering material for this purpose. While she worked on the Alangan language, she could also help survey other tribes nearby. Which areas were most in need of missionaries? What was the central point to work from? This was one of those times when, for five months, Hazel would be on a station by herself. That meant she had accounts to keep. What amount of money was spent on food? On mission supplies? On travel? Hazel always did a meticulous job of keeping records. Her conscience would not allow her to teach concepts to the tribal people that she herself didn't practise. At one time she went before the Lord to repent for not tithing her full ten-percent. Then she paid what was lacking.

This Alangan survey took her south and west of Calapan by truck, jeepney and on foot. Once more Hazel pushed hard, going beyond the call of duty to gather as much information as she could before the Mindoro Conference in October, 1954. The data she put together helped the language committee make necessary revisions in the Tagalog course of study. After fall conference, Caroline Stickley joined Hazel at Bayanan, and in November they made a trip to contact Alangan who had never heard the Gospel. At their first river crossing Hazel lost her shoes. Should they waste time going back? Hazel had travelled barefoot many times before, so she decided to go on without them. It was actually easier to keep the leeches off, but thorns and ants got a better hold. Her feet quickly toughened up, and often it was a benefit to be able to dig her toes into the ground. After all, these tribal people never wore shoes.

Hazel and Caroline had their usual bedding, mosquito net, medicines, food, clothing, phonograph and records. They were pleased to find an Alangan guide to take them further up the mountain. They were a bit disappointed as they approached one isolated Alangan home. Three forms jumped down from the back of the house and disappeared into the woods. "The people are afraid of your light-coloured clothes," the guide informed them. While he went to find the people who had disappeared, the girls changed into darker clothes. Within an hour about ten people had gathered, the men wearing G-strings and the women with rattan skirts. Hazel was intrigued by the women's unusual tops made from the leaves of a cactus plant, with the thorns removed. The leaves were held beside a bed of hot coals until they were dry and white. Then, while they were still flexible, the women sewed them together around their bodies with a narrow strip of vine.

This group was happy. They laughed a lot but still listened attentively to the Tagalog and Mangyan records, even though they didn't understand the Mangyan ones. Late in the afternoon the girls were ushered to a house, large enough to house twelve families during harvest. Built on stilts, with a high steep roof, it now housed only eight families, since harvest was finished. Under the house were small enclosures for little pigs. The evening was festive as they sang together, played records, and explained the Word until quite late. Even then the people were reluctant to go to bed. They would build a house for the missionaries if they would come and live there. If only they could! The next morning the girls were again chasing tiny, wild forest cockroaches. Hazel described it as the most interesting trip they had had for a long time. They took a host of souvenirs home to Bayanan with them—almost fifty cockroaches in Caroline's eyeglass case.

When Caroline left for her holiday, Betty Paeth came to help Hazel in Bayanan. Daily Vacation Bible School was a positive childhood memory for the missionaries, but they had never tried it here. This just seemed to be the right time. They printed Bible verses on the backs of used birthday and Christmas cards. They used Sunday school papers from Canada, with colourful Bible story pictures, as prizes for memorisation. The children had a delightful time. Betty went with Hazel on another trip to the Alangan, "four nights and five days in a new clean house with no cockroaches!"

# CHAPTER 12

## THE ALANGAN

"Twenty-two years have gone since Florence went to be with the Lord and it has been that long since I came to know Christ as my Saviour," Hazel wrote in a letter home. "I'm sure in many ways my growth in grace must be a disappointment to my Lord, but I have come to know Him better and want Him to control me always. I realise more and more how frail I am and how mighty He is. His power is mine as I claim it."

In every place of ministry Hazel's initial teachings began with *100 Questions Answered From the Bible*. In this way the Gospel was presented and the new believers discipled. These lessons covered all the doctrines needed for Christian living. What the people heard, they obeyed. On the Sunday they studied "Thou Shalt Not Steal," the response was wholehearted. One by one they came forward in obedience to give the Lord His share. One man brought his hen, which had just started to lay eggs. Hazel wisely suggested that he take care of it, sell the eggs and give that money to the Lord. On the Sunday they studied about adultery, a married man came after the service, broken and weeping, asking if God had forgiven all his sins. He had suddenly been convicted of his immoral lifestyle of the past. He was counselled to thank God that even his sin of adultery had been forgiven by Jesus' death. He went home rejoicing in the Lord.

Morning and afternoon, most of the people would come to listen to the records and to learn spiritual truths. That was why Hazel was there. She took every opportunity to teach them daily living, but it was an ongoing battle. These people were spiritual babes in Christ, needing constant care and guidance. One day Hazel noticed a child wearing a necklace of little wooden objects. The father explained that it was to keep the child from getting sick. Hazel gently brought correction. By using such things, she explained, he was taking his faith from the Lord and putting it in things that have no power. The next time she saw the child the objects were gone. When she wasn't there, things like this went unquestioned. Every time she went on a holiday for a couple of weeks or on furlough for a whole year, the people struggled spiritually. On the other hand, every word of Scripture she translated, and every record that was produced would be available to the people long after she left.

In case anyone in the homeland had any wrong ideas about the vacations she took, Hazel assured them that, along with the preaching and translation, there were cooking, laundry, carpentry and the usual household affairs. All this, along with winding the gramophone, teaching Scripture verses, singing hymns, praying with people and treating the sick, ensured her days were full. There were reasons the Mission was strict about scheduling in vacation time. Baguio, Luzon, was the vacation retreat for the missionaries, a beautifully cool spot in the Philippines about five and a half hours from Manila by bus. Hazel spent most of her annual holidays there (this year in May), enjoying the company of other missionaries on holiday. She hiked, wrote letters, read books, worked on her stamp collection, sewed and shopped. But no matter how wonderful a holiday was, Hazel was always eager to return to her tribal people. She often returned with trepidation, wondering what they had faced while she was gone.

Hazel was needed in the south again with the Buhid. This trip was different. She was to help Marie Barham and Russell Reed gather material for Buhid records. Carrying the recording equipment and batteries on their backs, along with other supplies, they went to Salcedo and on out to Manihala. Two Buhid men, who had previously helped translate some of the Scriptures for the records, now appeared again at just the right time, obviously sent by the Lord. These men read the prepared scripts in their language. The Lord kept the machine working. When the tapes were edited to the right length for the records, they had enough material recorded for seven sides of records. Hazel, Marie, Russell and the Buhid people were thrilled when it was finally all sent away. Now they just had to wait for the records to arrive.

Recorded messages in the local languages were vital, because the people were so wary of visitors. Lowlanders were always trying to take over the land where the Mangyan had lived all their lives. Then there was always the threat of having their children taken away to school. The record could be sent into secluded areas and the Gospel presented in a non-threatening way.

The Naujan, on the coast South of Calapan, was one group Hazel hoped to reach. One day, lowlanders, who wanted the Mangyan land, stopped Hazel and her guides! They did not want the missionaries to make contact with the Naujan. Hazel was relieved to have a letter of permission from the Governor with her. The lowlanders had no choice but to allow Hazel permission to travel in the area. This trip was to get a list of Taga Kaliwa words. Taga Kaliwa means "those of the left side." Rumour was that there were only about seventy-five people of this dialect left, and most spoke Tagalog. Hazel's group continued up the mountain, climbing to 1300 feet, down into the valley and up again and down, finally arriving at beautiful Lake Naujan. A one-hour boat trip brought them to a village, where Hazel got the same word list as the day before. But it wasn't a wasted trip. At least they knew what these people spoke. Word lists were also obtained from the Bangon and the Tadyawan.

Another trip took Hazel to the Sobaan River, which they followed and crossed about thirty times, then along a tributary, and up a dark forest trail. When they arrived at a tiny village, Here, Hazel found a very progressive group. They had better houses, lights of pitch wrapped in leaves, hammocks of bamboo, and handmade instruments. After the people listened to the Mangyan records, Hazel asked for a list of their words. They were Tadyawan and also understood the Naujan records made by Gospel Recordings.

Little by little the entire area was covered and various dialects pinpointed. All this was background work for when missionaries could move into these areas. After being out over a month, they had contacted five different groups: Alangan, Sori, Taga Kaliwa, Tadyawan and Bangon. Their general locations were now on record, and a number of their homes had been visited. By the end of May 1955, there were resident missionaries working with the Alangan people and others assigned to the Tadyawan.

It was a day of celebration—May 8, 1955, the first anniversary of Sunday services in Bayanan. OMF representatives were there: Mr. L. Porter, from South Africa, Mr. J. Kuhn, acting Regional Director from Singapore, and Dr. Broomhall, acting Superintendent in Calapan. Each gave a short message, and Hazel interpreted for the first time.

In contrast, May 18 was chaotic, to say the least. Hazel was moving out of the small house in Bayanan and Caroline was moving in. Hazel's new co-worker, Morven Brown, had arrived and would be moving with Hazel to the Alangan village of Ayan Bukug. Each of them had their own grocery supplies. Hazel sorted her things into bundles about the weight she could carry and placed them on the ground under the house, along with Morven's belongings. That made room for Caroline to move into the house.

When four men arrived to carry their supplies to Ayan Bukug, one man picked up Hazel's trunk and said, "Light! Add more." He was satisfied only when it was completely full. Of course, the most precious items in the load were the phonograph and records. When they arrived at Ayan Bukug, the men immediately sat down. They would not move until the phonograph was unpacked, so that they could listen to the records. The next day they had to hear both Tagalog and Iraya records again, before they would go to their fields.

"When will there be records in our language?"

"As soon as you help the missionaries learn the language!" That had to wait. First Hazel and Morven had to cut a path down the hill, dig a hole for garbage and another hole for their toilet. They arranged their boxes and shelves inside their house, and cut back the jungle until they could see tiny buses and cars creeping along the distant highway, ships on the ocean, and Calapan far below. Then they planted flower seeds from Morven's mother and some from Calapan. Hazel was determined to have flowers and vegetables, even if it meant putting up fences to keep out pigs, goats and chickens. Her letters home told how her flowers were growing and what fruits and vegetables they were eating. Her father, in turn, kept her up-to-date on what was growing in Victoria. But language study was a priority for them.

Manila! It became a joke in the mission that single missionary girls went to the dentist in Manila to meet boy friends. It had happened several times and resulted in marriage. Now Hazel was in Manila to take part in the wedding of Joy Hayman and Bob Hanselman. Joy must have married the last available man, because Hazel wrote her mother, "I don't see how this could happen to me with no single men now." It was a good thing Hazel could laugh about it. Sometimes well-meaning supporters wrote saying that they were praying for her to meet "a nice clergyman" or "a Spirit-filled lover!"

Morven stayed in Manila for a bit, so Hazel was alone in Ayan Bukug, but she was never really alone. Each morning, as soon as the sun was up, voices echoed through the jungle. The children were bathing in the stream below their house before coming to learn. They would come up dripping wet, but clean, with even their hair combed. The little boys wore G-strings and the girls wore only rattan skirts, so their clean bodies were their fresh clothes for the morning. They reminded one another if anyone forgot. It was an excellent spiritual example. God wanted to clean them up inside (take their sins away), and wanted His home (their bodies) to be clean. The children soon learned that if Jesus lived in their hearts, their thoughts, words and deeds would be clean, as well. Hazel bathed like everyone else, with her dirty clothes on, lathering under them, rinsing off, walking home dripping wet and then changing into clean clothes.

Inside Hazel's home, the children would settle on their haunches to work on reading lessons, their almost bare brown bodies gleaming. Ranak, a little older and wearing a shirt and shorts, was the star reader. He learned quickly. Hazel was delighted when he used his own money to buy a Bible and a pencil so that he could learn to write.

One day Morven asked the age of a certain child. The father began to count, "*One, two, three, four,*" pointing and looking in a different direction at each count. "The child is four years old," he replied. Then he explained to them how he knew. "When the boy was born, I had my rice field over there. The next year my field was up on that hill. Last year it was down lower, and this year my rice field is there across the stream. That makes the boy four years old."

"How old is your girl?"

"Twelve," he answered at once.

"Why didn't you count your fields like you did for the other child?"

"Because the time I got medicine for her in Bayanan you asked me how old she was, and I counted them then."

"How old are you?"

"We remember only for our own children. When they marry, we don't bother remembering anymore. I must be fifty." Fifty, and just learning for the first time about the Saviour. These people had so much to learn, and they longed for records in their own language so that the people could learn faster.

Tithing was one thing they did learn well, and the missionaries puzzled over what to do with all of the rice and other produce the people brought. Then the Lord gave wisdom. If the people wanted records in their own language, one or two of their number could help translate the scripts. They would be paid with the rice that was brought for offerings. That worked! In one week, tribal translators helped Morven and Hazel translate six scripts each for gospel records. The next step before recording them was to check the scripts with other Alangan. Hazel also translated her sermon and two choruses into the Alangan language. The people enjoyed the choruses. Hazel was now the chairman of the OMF Linguistic Committee and had added correspondence to do.

Within a year of their first visit to Ayan Bukug, Hazel and Morven were living there. Alangan songs were being used in the Sunday service, the first Alangan sermons were preached, and several people had assurance of sins forgiven and were witnessing to others. They were eagerly awaiting records in their own language, so they could reach others.

"When these words are on records, our friends in Alangan will be very happy. But who will take the phonograph and wind it for them?" Ranak asked.

"Wouldn't you like to do it?" Hazel asked him. "In this way you could serve God." The missionaries' constant desire was that their spiritual children would go on with the Lord and reach out to others.

Rosario and Anghel

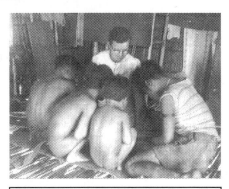

Ranak and friends learn to read.

# CHAPTER 13

## TO THE BUHID

Morven and Hazel were pleased when the people in Ayan Bukug decided to build them a better house, and they were impressed with the care that went into making it. Kabunang, the leader, was a true believer, and most of those helping were as well, but their motive was not always clear. Which was more important, spiritual teaching or the medicine provided by Morven, a nurse? Both were vital.

Late one dark night the girls heard voices in the jungle. They could see torch lights bobbing along the path. Something must be wrong, they thought, and they were right. It was unusual for Morven to be called to attend to the sick at night, but a man with severe TB was having difficulty breathing. Morven took her supplies and went with them, while one young lad stayed with Hazel. Not knowing what was happening, Hazel prayed as the time passed.

Suddenly a burst of loud laughter floated across the jungle trees. Morven was still chuckling when she returned. All the people had gathered around the man, where he lay on the porch of a flimsy house. Morven knew they would all want to watch her give the man a penicillin injection. Just as she leaned over to plunge the needle into the man's skin, the porch began to wobble. It not only wobbled, it collapsed! Morven felt herself falling, when one of the women grabbed her by the hair. Morven was bruised but not hurt, and they all had a hearty laugh together. After five injections over the next few days, the man was well enough to go home.

The New Year of 1956 started off with many reasons to celebrate. Young Ranak read a simple Bible story in Tagalog in church while the missionaries were away. Days later the new House of God in Bayanan was dedicated, with over one hundred Mangyan and several Tagalog people attending the occasion. It was amazing to consider that two years earlier not one of them had known the Saviour. The following Sunday, twenty-five were out to the service in Ayan Bukug, and after the closing prayer, two of the believers spontaneously led out in prayer for the first time in their lives. All of these events were so encouraging!

Hazel and Morven went back to Calapan to prepare and record the scripts for Alangan records. This was an exciting but intense job. José Punto was chosen to do the actual speaking on the tape, so he practised all day with the girls, repeating every phrase. Every word had to be correct. Many of the spiritual teachings being recorded were new to José. The walls of the buildings were paper-thin, and Calapan was a busy, noisy place during the day, so they decided to do the recording late at night. José was so interested and pleased with the message that sometimes when a sentence was read to him, he would exclaim, "How good!" They would remind him that he was to repeat the phrase so it could be put on the records. Later, when another phrase was read to him, he would exclaim, "Really?" Again they would explain the process to him. It was a joy and a relief when the recordings were finally on their way to Gospel Recordings in Los Angeles. Along with the recordings went a request that they be processed as soon as possible. They needed them for their trips during the dry season, March to June.

While the people learned the Word, Hazel was constantly learning about interesting creatures in the jungle, such as "jumping leeches." Striped and larger than other leeches, they hung in the foliage at head height. They would jump on the head of an unsuspecting passer-by, inch their way to the eyeball, and inject their blood-thinner, resulting in a red, itchy eye. Thankfully, Hazel didn't learn that by experience!

One place Hazel wanted to reach with the Gospel was Baksing. When she asked Narding if she could walk the nine and a half hours with him to Baksing, she had no idea of the highs and lows awaiting her there. But every life situation, even the difficult ones, became an opportunity to teach the Word of God. One day five people gave their hearts to the Lord. That same evening, a baby became very ill. Hazel did everything she could for the little one. She cared for the baby all night, using all of her medical experience, but the next morning the baby died. Suddenly all kinds of heathen practices were in conflict with Christian concepts. Would the parents allow a Christian funeral? They agreed, then quietly buried the child without telling Hazel.

One by one the people were turning from darkness to light. Two more people opened their hearts to Christ. On Sunday several more accepted Christ. These new babes in Christ desperately needed teaching--from the basic concept of salvation, to baptism, to daily living. But Hazel had to return to Ayan Bukug. It pained her to leave these new Christians all alone.

The long-awaited Gospel records finally arrived. They would be dynamic in spreading the Word and in teaching new believers. Hazel almost wept when she opened the parcel. Over half of the one hundred records had been broken in shipping! By this time Frances had gone on furlough, and she and Hazel were the only ones who had studied the Iraya language. Hazel went to her knees. She felt pulled to leave the Alangan work and offer to work among the Iraya people, but right now she was preparing about twenty Alangan believers in Ayan Bukug for baptism. This had been an interesting process. Baptism classes couldn't be taught until the catechism dealing with this topic was translated so that the people could understand. She did that first. Once the believers were all properly instructed, each candidate would be examined to make sure his or her testimony of salvation was clear and their motivation was strictly obedience.

Obedience in baptism was always an indication that a person was serious about following the Lord. It was a wonderful day, a milestone, when finally thirteen new believers at Ayan Bukug were baptised: four men, four women, three young men, and two girls.

Baptism was followed with fellowship around the Lord's table. This was the first time that the Lord's Supper was served at Ayan Bukug. For Hazel this was one of the most difficult doctrines to explain. She used all the Alangan she knew, as well as explaining it in simple Tagalog, but some still couldn't totally understand.

It was hard to believe what had taken place here in Ayan Bukug in only one year: the first Christmas, the first Alangan records, first primer, first readers and writers. Forty people regularly gathered for Bible study. Now instead of singing pagan lullabies to their children, they sang hymns. The older children sang hymns during their play. People would meet for prayer before going on trips and give thanks before their meals. Some even led in prayer in public meetings without embarrassment.

With Hazel as their teacher, it wasn't surprising that the believers at Ayan Bukug had a missionary vision of reaching others. Kabunang took an all-day trip to visit other Alangan and returned happy that some were responsive and wanted to hear the records. As a result, the believers at Ayan Bukug purchased a phonograph to use in outreach. Oh, yes, the records. Alangan records had arrived at Calapan but were sent back to Manila to see if the astronomically high duty could be reduced. Some records had been sent by mistake to the Reeds on the other side of the island. How do you explain all that red tape to tribal people? When the records finally did arrive at Ayan Bukug, the people were ecstatic.

"Can't we hear the Alangan records?" Kabunang asked, as Hazel sat down to enjoy a drink of water.

"Perhaps this afternoon," she teased him. He looked closely at her to see if she really meant that, so she quickly added, "If you take the ties off the box, perhaps we could hear one record." The people giggled in a pleased manner. At the end of the record Kabunang stated that it was true Alangan.

"These all sound like Punto," he said, after hearing the second record. "Where are the ones that Sumisinay and Mariano Lakoy helped with?" Hazel had to explain that even though they had helped with some of the words, it was easier to have only one person say them all into the machine. They were disappointed that they would not hear their friends on the records, but they were not disappointed in the messages.

Only days later the church commissioned two of the men, Kabunang and Bodangtu, to the Lord's service. Clad in their G-strings and carrying small baskets of belongings, they prayed together and then set out on a missionary journey to tell other people about the Lord. Kabunang returned a week later with the news that several people were ready to follow the Lord. The next time he visited them, he would take the phonograph and records!

While some believers stood firm, Hazel was disappointed when other believers fell into sin. The truth of the Word couldn't be taught quickly enough. If a spouse died and a man needed a mother for his children, there was no concept of Christian marriage. Many of the people didn't even adhere to their own cultural ethics. There were not enough missionaries to go around. When a fellow missionary got sick or died, it was keenly felt. A cloud of sadness hung over all of them when John Thompson was stricken with polio. The whole missionary family pulled together in prayer. Thankfully, he was in Manila when he got sick, not in a tribal region. They would all work hard to fill the void.

The new records helped. Often, when waiting for buses or jeepneys, people asked Hazel to play the records. Wherever she stayed, the phonograph would be played late into the night. When Hazel gave Punto a phonograph and records to use, he sometimes didn't get "night" at all. Every place he stopped the people wanted to listen to the records.

There was no rest for the records and little rest for him. The people were keen to learn.

Sometimes lessons were learned at a high price. The tribal people had developed an ingenious way to hunt wild pig for food. Bait was laid out with a trip line. When a pig tripped the line, an arrow would catapult through the air, killing the pig. Signs beside the trails warned when a pig trap was set up. Parents warned their children and built a big log fence to keep the children away. One day a brother and sister were out gathering sepsepen, a special fruit. They disobeyed and crossed the fence and Totowan, the little girl, triggered the trip line. The bamboo arrow went right through the little girl's abdomen, from one hipbone to the other. The parents pushed the intestines back in, tied bark-cloth around the wound and delivered her to Hazel. Hazel treated her for shock, but there was nothing she could do. Totowan died.

The little girl had been bright in her faith in the Lord. All night there were people in the house. They prayed, sang, and talked. Hazel read the Word, and the next morning they buried Totowan in the children's graveyard. Her father, a new believer, was almost prostrate with grief. He wanted to be buried, too. Only prayer and the continual reading of God's Word day after day brought him peace. Gradually his faith grew strong again. According to their culture, they would remember her for nine years. The missionaries comforted and wept with the people even as they taught.

As Hazel prepared for her furlough, she also prepared more believers for baptism. A man, a woman, and five young boys, ages ten to fourteen, were baptised before she left. The first elders had been chosen for the Alangan church, Kabunang and Mariano Lakoy. Hazel was relieved that this time the believers would not be left alone. Beverly Erickson was assigned to join Morven, so the teaching among the Alangan would continue.

It was interesting to realise, as Hazel got her American visa and Canadian passport renewed in 1957, that this would be her first official furlough. What she did on this furlough would set a precedent for the years ahead. The ship's crew was Chinese, so she had fun trying to recall that language. They seemed to understand her Chinese better than she understood their English. She also gave them a variety of tracts and Scripture in their language, from the supply she always had with her. Hazel's habit of *eating her way through the menu* delighted the kitchen crew. At times she was the only passenger on board with an appetite. During this trip she wrote over forty thank-you letters to people back in the Philippines. She played Scrabble and usually could find a place to skip rope for exercise. Stamp collectors seem to have a way of discovering each other, and Hazel was always ready to do some serious trading.

Considering all she went through when she left China, going through Customs and Immigration now never worried her. Back in Canada, she endured the usual routine of medical and dental checkups and whatever procedures were needed to bring everything up to par. OMF required all their missionaries to represent the Mission at various conferences. Except for being apart from her parents, this was no hardship for Hazel. She loved to talk about her work. Times at home with her parents became more and more precious, though, as the years passed. Hazel was well aware that any one of their partings could be their last; sometimes it was difficult to say good-bye even for short trips during her furlough.

Hazel covered Canada from coast to coast—Victoria to Halifax—on every furlough. She never missed People's Church in Toronto. From that very first commitment at Saskatoon Bible College, People's Church had faithfully kept their part of the bargain, supporting her the entire time she was on the mission field. Hazel knew the Women's Missionary Group at People's Church prayed faithfully for her, and were always pleased to have her there.

Hazel visited retired missionaries and parents of other OMF missionaries. She took the "family aspect" of the Mission seriously and kept in touch with missionaries who had left the Philippines and visited them whenever she could, like John Thompson and his family and Myra Lou Barnard who had been seriously burned in the Philippines when a kerosene tank exploded. This she did, as well as visiting her own financial and prayer supporters. She also visited her aunts, uncles and cousins. If she couldn't actually see someone in person, she talked to him or her by phone. Attending OMF conferences and speaking to various church groups, missionary fellowships and even the occasional school were taken in stride. But most of all she loved talking to the various groups in her own church.

"The support of each missionary and the whole work of the Fellowship is provided through the freewill offerings of individuals, groups, and churches in answer to prayer," was the OMF policy. "Needs are made known only in response to specific inquiry. We make no public appeal for funds." This was OMF policy, and Hazel adhered to it without question. Never once did she make an appeal for funds, and she never lacked financially. In fact, she usually was given more money personally than she needed as she travelled. Hazel was meticulous in managing her money, using it only where it was designated and accounting for all of it.

The missionary allowance for living expenses included home-assignment travel, housing, local travel, the missionary's share of administration, personal allowance and retirement provision. The evidence of the Lord's hand on a person was believed to be in direct proportion to the growth of their support team, churches and individuals. It was very obvious that His hand was upon Hazel, as her list of supporters grew.

Because of her involvement with Wycliffe, Hazel was often asked to teach at their SIL, either in Grand Forks, North Dakota, or at Caronport, Saskatchewan. She loved meeting people she knew from past SIL courses and making new friends. While she might possibly teach one linguistics class a day, she could also monitor several others to keep up with the new methods of teaching. But Hazel's favourite conference was at The Firs, at Bellingham, WA, close enough that her parents could sometimes go with her. With this much to do, a year at home flew by.

"It seems hard to believe I'll not see them (her parents) for another five years," Hazel said when the time came for her to return to the field. Even before she boarded the ship she was writing letters home. "Sorry I've left so much stuff not put away in my room. There is space in my trunk and if you like you can put things in it instead of in the suitcases. The papers can go in the attic if you like." The attic was accessed via a ladder through a trapdoor in her parents' bedroom ceiling. She knew how difficult going to the attic was for her ageing parents. She had intended to clean the attic while she was home. It still wasn't done when she left.

If Hazel thought things would slow down once she got back to the Philippines in March of 1958, she was mistaken. A new assignment awaited her. She and Betty Paeth were to make an extensive trip into the interior of the northeast part of Mindoro to find out how many Iraya people didn't understand and speak Tagalog and needed a translation. This assignment was tailor-made for Hazel. It combined her love for travel, her love for linguistics, and her love for the Iraya people. She was ready to go. She had walked miles and climbed flights and flights of stairs in Canada to keep in shape. She knew that there would not be time to work up to jungle trekking once she was back on the field, and she didn't want to waste a minute.

Starting from Kaagutayan, Hazel and Betty climbed for six hours to Batino, 1200 feet above sea level. One of their guides for this trip remembered meeting Hazel at Kaagutayan four years earlier. She was so pleased. There was a hunger for the Word of God in Batino, and although only two people had been baptised, many more had already trusted the Lord. Another three hours over more rugged hills brought them to Camurong and another friendly welcome. For six evenings they met with Christians, prayed, taught and sang. Gradually they worked their way up higher, to 3900 feet and then 5300 feet. They had climbed to the very top of the mountain range that cut the island in half! They could see the ocean beyond the northwest coast.

By conference time Hazel and Betty had gathered enough information to know the Iraya translation was needed. They found many Iraya people in the interior who did not understand Tagalog. That report was taken to conference to help in the decision-making process. The Mission family—fifty-two missionaries and their children—enjoyed the fellowship, services, prayer meetings, the Lord's Supper, and business meetings at the conference. The highly anticipated event, though, was when new assignments were announced. Everyone, including Hazel, waited eagerly. Hopefully, she would be reassigned to the Iraya people.

# CHAPTER 14

## THE HANUNOO

Hazel and Elly van der Linden were designated to the Hanunoo area of southeast Mindoro. Hazel's greatest love was the Iraya people, but they were in good hands. Frances Williamson was assigned to work on the translation of the Scriptures in the Iraya language. Hazel was going to use her linguistic abilities with yet another tribe. It was an exciting challenge.

The Hanunoo, a large tribal group of five to six thousand people, stayed strictly to their language. Translation here was going to be a challenge for Hazel and Elly, because the Hanunoo had developed their own script, not letters, but characters, which they carved on bamboo strips. A good percentage of both young and old could read. The Hanunoo believers wanted a Bible in that script. By June 1958, Hazel and Elly were preparing to make teaching records for these people to help them learn doctrine. Hazel wrote to Mr. Holder at Central Baptist Church in Victoria, B.C. "On our last trip in the mountains we spent almost two weeks with the Hanunoo people. We were encouraged ... to find there is a good percentage of literacy as far as reading their own script is concerned, both among women and men as well as some of the older children. We have written to the American Bible Society office in Manila to see if they would consider printing portions of the Bible in the Hanunoo script. We expect that within the next two months we can get some simple translation work done to leave as we go from place to place." She concluded that the money the Central Baptist Church had sent would be used for this purpose.

The culture in this southern area of Mindoro was quite different in several ways. Here they grew cotton, spun thread, and wove their own cloth for the women's skirts and men's G-strings. Beautifully embroidered designs decorated their clothes and woven baskets. Both men and women had long hair. They also had the most interesting three-stringed instrument, much like a violin, with strings and bow made of human hair. These people were keen to learn. They would ask for story after story and said that they could go on listening all night. They were also very honest in pointing out Hazel's mistakes. That was fine. Hazel welcomed correction. She didn't want any mistakes in her translations!

After forty-one days with the Hanunoo, Hazel and Elly had gathered enough information to take to Manila, to the Institute of National Languages. Dr. Alejandro analysed the information. He felt that it was important to give these people the Gospel in their own script. Hazel and Elly were thrilled.

There was a major problem, though, one that Hazel had never before encountered. Every character in the Hanunoo script was a combination of consonant and vowel. In speaking they could end words with a consonant, but in writing they couldn't do that, because the consonants and vowels were combined. They would just leave off the entire character, and even the people were confused.

In translating Scriptures, confusion had to be eliminated. Hazel was puzzling over that when Dr. Alejandro showed her an example of the ancient Tagalog script. Years earlier, when Catholic priests were translating the ancient Tagalog script, they found there were no final consonants in that script either. They solved the problem by adding final consonant-vowel combinations, but underlining them to indicate that they were final and the vowel was to be dropped. Dr. Alejandro suggested that the girls try this with the Hanunoo script.

When they got back to Hanunoo territory, Hazel chose verses already translated, and wrote them in their script. Using Dr. Alejandro's idea, she underlined characters for finals and explained to the people how it worked. The people then had no trouble reading them. Hazel was greatly relieved.

By the end of August, only months after beginning work with the Hanunoo, Hazel had the story of Zacchaeus written up to read to the people. She and Elly took turns every other day sharing the Word, and the rest of the time they studied the language. Whenever anyone came to visit, they ferreted out new words. Their list quickly grew to over two thousand words besides the names of people and places.

Hazel and Elly visited the Hanunoo village of Sinariri, where six believers had already been baptised. "We perceived … a hunger, which far exceeded our teaching ability in Hanunoo. We are all the more urged to study with all our might." They began praying for a house in Sinariri so they could spend more time there teaching. As well as working on the Hanunoo language, they had five Tagalog-speaking centres: Bulalacao, Binli, Tarubong, Sinariri and Mansalay, where they ministered, two weeks at a time at each place. This meant long periods between visits. They prayed that God would send help, so that they could concentrate on the Hanunoo.

The girls were not yet familiar with the landmarks in this mountainous jungle area, but a guide wasn't always available when they needed one. That was frustrating. Finally Hazel and Elly decided to make the trip to Sinariri without a guide. About noon they realised that they had meandered off on the wrong trail. A young man in a nearby house showed them the way back. Later they arrived at a river, and quickly realised it was not the one they were looking for. Which way should they go? They wandered around and it was almost dark when they came upon an empty house in a field. The floor of the house was so tiny that their feet were off the end when they lay down, but they were glad for shelter overhead. In the morning, thankfully, someone finally came along and showed them the way.

On another trip, Nik Wehren accompanied them, again without a guide, but Nik planned to ask directions all along the way. That trip took them ten hours, because they stopped so often to ask directions. It did offer them excellent opportunities to speak with people, and their walking time was actually only six hours.

Serafim, their guide on another trip, took it upon himself to explain to people at one stop what hell was like. "It's like if you were trying to cross a flooded river and you kept on swimming and swimming and you could see the bank ahead of you like a big wall you couldn't climb," he explained. "You got more weary all the time and wished you could get out or else give in and drown but you couldn't do either. But the difference is that in hell the water will be fire and you will suffer in it forever." The other side of the picture, the gospel of salvation and the hope of heaven, was quickly presented.

"Where did you first see the Bible?" Serafim asked Hazel.

Hazel explained that in her country Bibles were easily obtained, and in her family each one had their own Bible from the time they were very young.

"When did you first accept the Lord?"

"Twenty-six years ago," was her answer. Hazel added in a letter home, "With the Mangyan it has only been two, three or four years since they first heard the Gospel. They have no Bible and have had limited teaching. What a great debt we owe them, we who have had the light for so long."

"Mansalay, Sinariri, Tarubong, Mansalay, Calapan, Manila, Calapan, Salcedo, Calapan, Ayan Bukug, Calapan, Mansalay, Sinariri, Binli, Bulalacao, Binli, Sinariri, Tarubong,

Mansalay, Sinariri, Binli, Bulalacao, Buyayaw, Mansalay. This is the order in which I lived at these places the past three months, a few days at a time. The longest was twelve days at Sinariri this last time when I was alone." (The girls had houses now in Mansalay, Sinariri, Tarubong and Binli.) When Doreen Hodgkinson joined Hazel and Elly in the Hanunoo work in November, 1958, it added to their workload at first—introducing her to the work and to language study—but in the long run, one more person meant more time for outreach.

One of Hazel's frustrations was that so many Christian principles were learned by the people by trial and error. They just couldn't teach the people fast enough to avoid some of the pitfalls of sin. One example was the day they sat in on a law case in Tarubong. The people killed a goat and cooked a big meal for the ones who came to the trial. Huliyu was on trial because he had two wives. He was fined eight arm-spans of double-strings of little white seed-beads. Plus, he had to put away his second wife. He and his wife Api were regarded as Christians, but a few days later Huliyu told Hazel he didn't think he had ever really accepted Christ before. He wanted to accept Him right then.

This year, again, Hazel had the joy of being present when people heard the Christmas story for the first time. The spiritually hungry people in Sinariri asked for more stories, naming some they had already heard. Hazel and Elly read for an hour. The people were so eager to learn that they could have listened for much longer. Hazel couldn't imagine being without the Word herself or being unable to read it.

Badyang was the ultimate work of God that every missionary longs to tell about. The Christians at Ayan Bukug took the Gospel to the village of Badyang. This was their mission field, and Palay was their main teacher. They had a fine crop of spiritual fruit, and twelve Christians wanted to be baptised. Kabunang, Mariano Lakoy and Palay, elders from Ayan Bukug, examined each of these twelve candidates in preparation for baptism. Hazel and two other missionaries were there to help only when asked. Two candidates were asked to wait because their understanding, motive or lifestyle (chewing the addictive betel nut), was not quite right. Some, who had previously been asked to wait, were now accepted for baptism. This spoke well for Palay's teaching. The missionaries were thrilled to see the local Christian men taking leadership and receiving guidance from the Lord.

As part of the Hanunoo study, the Mission now needed to find out about the people west of the mountains. Dr. Broomhall was well acquainted with Hazel. He knew that she was fearless, healthy, single, and knew what she was looking for. She would be the perfect person for the job. So Hazel was sent out on another trip, this time to track down the Gubatnon and Ratagnon peoples. These tribes were in the south of Mindoro, but west of the mountains. This trip would push her to the limits of physical endurance, but Hazel loved the challenge. The Gubatnon people she contacted listened over and over to the Hanunoo records and seemed to understand them. She concluded that with a few slight changes, these people spoke the Hanunoo language. The Ratagnon were not so easy to locate, and a list of their words seemed to indicate a new language. The trip ended with no clear number of how many people were in that group. Frustrating!

In May 1959, Hazel and three others set out a second time to contact the Ratagnon. At their first stop, no one wanted to give her Ratagnon words. At a home farther on, they finally received a list almost exactly like the others. It was supposedly part Visayan. The news that they were spending the night in Banban spread quickly. Early in the morning, people began to come and by 7:00 A.M. there were over thirty adults and their children. They worshipped and read the Word for two hours, and even then the people lingered.

All their names were written down, as usual, to find out how many people were in each area. Each one eagerly asked to have his name listed. Hazel explained carefully that having their names on this list wouldn't save them. This could happen only if their names were in the Book of Life in Heaven. Some said that they had never heard of the salvation through Christ. Others said they believed the first time they heard. Hazel had only Psalm 23 in Hanunoo to leave for those who could read. The phonograph had a broken spring, so the records couldn't be used.

Hazel left with a heavy heart. The people didn't have the Word to feed on, and no one to teach them more until she could return. The Ratagnon was fast decreasing as a tribal language group, partly due to the high mortality rate, as well as intermarriage with the Hanunoo and Visayan of the area. The people claimed that the oldest Ratagnon spoke the same language as the rest but used an older form when they spoke among themselves.

Ann Flory was designated to join their Hanunoo team in September. Hazel had taught her in Philadelphia and knew she would learn the language quickly. Elly was scheduled to go home the following April. Doreen married Nik Wehren in 1959, and they moved to San Isidru, a new work among the Gubatnan. By now, Hazel had over twelve hundred sentences written out and twice as many more to classify, write out and learn. It was time to begin another dictionary. There were difficult portions of this language that she discovered when working on a message on the body of Christ. In Hanunoo there was no way to say that the toe is a member of the body. They say, there are many names for the body, and one is the toe. Her mind raced to find a good way of saying something she took for granted in English.

Hazel also had language work to check from missionaries working in the Buhid, Batangan and Iraya tribes. But when an opportunity arose to get Scriptures recorded by the Bible Society on three-minute records, she dropped everything. This was by far the best way to reach and teach the people. They had to check what had already been translated and prepare it for recording. There was a deadline. Hazel knew how to meet deadlines.

114

It seemed as if her life was always in a rush but sometimes she just had to stop. "Lately I have been especially conscious of God's care for me," Hazel wrote home in December of that year. "The other morning in Mansalay I stopped quickly as I reached into the bag of bread on top of the cupboard. Only a few inches above my head hung a loop of the body of a boa constrictor." This was one problem Hazel would not look after herself. She recruited a neighbour to get rid of the snake.

Hazel was in Bulalacao, trying to get to sleep. A typhoon raged outside but that was not unusual. What she didn't appreciate was that the place was infested with bedbugs. She decided to sleep on the floor and was soon drifting off to sleep. Suddenly the typhoon lifted the ridge covering off the roof. Hazel moved to the sitting room. Off to sleep again and all at once a whole sheet of corrugated roofing was airborne. She had no choice now but the kitchen floor. In that storm their Mansalay house was left leaning on the house next to it. Their Tarubong house had its roof and floors lifted and walls partly removed. The house in Sinariri was flattened. All their possessions, though few, were scattered out in the rain. The only house standing fairly erect was the one in Binli. As senior worker in the area now, Hazel had the responsibility of overseeing both volunteers and hired help. Repairing houses, whether damaged by storm or ageing, took time but it had to be done. Hazel would much rather be translating Scriptures.

Christmas this year would be very busy. They were hosting the annual Believers' Conference at Tarubong. It was always a time of spiritual growth for the tribal church that hosted it. This annual conference had started out small but now over one hundred Christians gathered from various areas to encourage and strengthen one another. As usual, some people came just for the food and slipped off after they ate. Others stayed and heard a good gospel message by Arsenio, interpreted by Huliyu. By the next morning, only the

Christians remained and that was the main reason for the conference, teaching the believers.

While Hazel took her holidays, Ann and Elly looked after the work in Binli and Tarubong. Ann finished her Tagalog studies and wrote her last test. Elly taught the believers about baptism and the Lord's Supper in preparation for baptisms. "We want to see only those who are truly born again baptised so the church among the Hanunoo may be kept with a good testimony which will bring glory to the Lord." Four men and one woman were baptized in Sinariri. It was a deeply moving experience when the new believers could celebrate the Lord's Supper for the first time right after their baptism, but they would have to wait for that because there was no one to serve it. OMF policy was that a man must serve the Lord's Supper. One solution would be to have a missionary man or a couple working in this area. Best of all would be for local church elders to perform this ceremony, but none of the local men were spiritually ready for that role.

Five men were baptised at Binli, and Tom Graumann came and served communion on the rocks of the riverbed. The men didn't even have to change clothes, since they wore only G-strings anyway. Two of the men led in prayers of thanks for the sweet potato used as bread and the coconut shell of water to represent the blood of the Lord. A few days later at Tarubong, two men and four women were baptised. This time boiled banana was used for the bread, and a cup of water represented the wine. Hazel shared the news in her letters that sixteen were baptised within two weeks.

The problem of who would serve the Lord's Supper was finally solved with the appointment of the Wehrens to the area. It was nice to have Doreen back, along with her husband. They took over the town house and village home and related ministry. This left Hazel and Elly with only four places to look after: a nice reprieve. Hazel purchased another typewriter in Manila, almost new. Between them they owned three typewriters and had one on loan, so now they had one in each of their four homes. A typewriter was essential for translation and correspondence. Having fewer pounds to carry with them made quite a difference on some trips.

"These folks still don't have even a whole Gospel to read, just small portions that they have helped us translate. Only a few can read well enough to get the sense of the spiritual truths so they have not been able to feed on the Word unless we are there to help them." Ann Flory was making good progress and was available to help Hazel when Elly went on furlough. Missionary terms on the field in 1960 were reduced to four years.

The Wehrens were a wonderful addition to the team working in that area. Like a close-knit family, they all happily anticipated the arrival of a baby in the Wehren home. But it wasn't just one baby, but two babies. The arrival of the Wehren twins meant that the family needed to be close to a doctor, so they were transferred to the Tagalog work in Mamburao. Ann and Hazel were back to looking after all six places again. Hazel was also busy working on Tadyawan and Iraya reports.

Hazel pushed hard to put together a simple Doctrinal Primer in Hanunoo for new readers. This was a long process. It had to be checked in each village and then typed. Then the Hanunoo script needed to be written for Lusiyanu and Banban folk that did not read Roman script. Hazel enlisted help, and by August of that year the first draft for twelve lessons was finished. How like the Lord to have these lessons prepared just in time to deal with a doctrinal issue.

One of the men in charge of the phonograph began to put his own interpretation on the Word. He would play the records for the people and then ask them who Jesus was. That was followed with his own interpretation: that Jesus was not God and they should worship only God the Father. He was ordered out of some homes and almost came to blows with some of the people. Hazel spent a good bit of time teaching him the truth from the Word and encouraging those he had tried to indoctrinate. She was so glad that doctrinal information had already been translated.

Another problem that had nothing to do with doctrine was their worship service. Hazel liked things done "decently and in order," and it bothered her a bit that in Binli there was no order. The people would speak up and correct the missionary's mistakes and, if they agreed or disagreed with what was being taught, they mentioned it. If they had an added testimony, they interrupted. There were some advantages to this, but Hazel would have preferred that this type of discussion would take place in a Sunday school class apart from a reverent worship service.

The records, such a vital part of their teaching, also caused some problems. Jealousy arose between relatives if the records were played longer in one home than in another. It was hard for them to understand that one person had to be responsible for the machine. When the phonograph broke, that problem was avoided for the time being, but it brought up another problem. "How can we worship on Sunday when our phonograph is broken?" Ribladu asked. Hazel was surprised by the question until she realised they had never had a meeting without it. That night Hazel taught Ribladu more about prayer and worship. The next Sunday they worshipped without records!

It wasn't only among the tribal people that things were tense at times. Hazel was frugal, and as a result, kept "things" she thought she might need some time. She was also focused. When she saw something that needed to be done, and the best way to do it, she didn't wait for others to catch up. Her co-workers often disagreed with her methods and the risks she took. It didn't bother her to be off in the jungle alone with the tribal people. Dr. Hogben finally gave her Carnegie's book, *How to Win Friends and Influence People.*

"He (Carnegie) surely makes clear how we need to give those we live with loving consideration and encourage and compliment them, allow them to talk about what is on their hearts," she wrote home. "I'm afraid I need to learn a lot along these lines so that I 'esteem others better than myself.' Pray that I may be all I should be in my relations with Ann and the people I work with."

# CHAPTER 15

## SHORT TERM BIBLE SCHOOLS

Short Term Bible Schools (STBS) were now emerging as a wonderful means of multiplying workers. Christian leaders could come from the surrounding areas for a whole week of teaching. In December 1960, Hazel and Ann were busy preparing for their first Short Term Bible School at Binli in the Hanunoo area. Hazel was putting together lessons on Galatians, Bible Doctrine, and First Aid. Meanwhile, Ann was preparing Bible stories for the children, a Bible Survey course, and health lessons. The week would end with a Christmas feast on Saturday. Hazel would teach a week at Sinariri, so that the people would know what to expect at a STBS. Hopefully, some would come with her to Binli.

Usig (who often helped with translation) cleared the ground under the roof of his unfinished house for a classroom. Others helped him, and they soon had four bamboo benches across the width of the house. At the front, they tied the large blackboard given by a lowlander interested in the Mangyan. So they had a chapel-without-walls finished before Hazel arrived with three students from Sinariri. Presidente, the Binli leader, made the three strangers feel right at home. The bell sounded about 6:30 A.M. on Tuesday for the first day of classes, but it was after 7:30 before they really began with singing and prayer. Forty-five adults and children enrolled, but the average attendance was thirty. Some arrived Wednesday from Tarubong, three more came on Thursday from Sinariri, and still others arrived on

Saturday from Tarubong for the feast and services. It made teaching somewhat difficult, but it was thrilling to see them come, if only for part of the week.

Hazel taught the study from Galatians, while Ann taught the children. Then Ann taught a health class. After recess they gathered for Bible Survey with Ann and ended the morning with Hazel's Reading Introduction Class. In the afternoon Hazel taught First Aid and Christian Life, while Ann had games with the children. Every one of these topics was of major importance. The same schedule was used each day except Friday. That day they had a testimony meeting.

Early Saturday morning a goat, several chickens, and vegetables were prepared. Huge pots of rice were cooked as the main part of the Christmas meal for them to share together. This was a great step of faith for the Binli Christians, since typhoons had vastly reduced their crops. They trusted the Lord to provide and He did.

Hazel was delighted when all eighty who came to the feast stayed for the meeting in the "chapel." It was not uncommon for people to come just for the food. This day was different. They sang together. Then Usig, with the help of Agin and Ambung, explained the "Human Heart" poster, and Hazel gave a short message.

Husi, one of Presidente's sons, showed an increased interest in the things of the Lord. Agin, who had just helped explain the "Human Heart" poster, mentioned he wanted to learn to read so that he could read God's Word. One by one, leaders were being raised up from among the people. The end of December introduced another milestone for the area. The new Hanunoo records arrived, with three Scripture portions on each side.

Always strong and robust, Hazel had to restrain herself when fellow missionaries visited. "They are not used to hiking in the mountains so we took almost eight hours instead of four or five to come from Manaul (to Binli). Really—the resting took the time. They had no idea the trails were so long and hard. It is good for them to know so they can pray better for us." With such a strong constitution, Hazel was not quite prepared for the results of her physical exam in January 1961. "I feel well but the doctors say these days at my age (44) they always like to take tests so they can be sure nothing is wrong." She could still out-walk and out-work everyone who came to work with her. Now she was in Manila, where more tests had been scheduled, including a D & C. Always present was the unspoken thought of cancer.

Hazel was relieved to know that Dr. Edward Glazier would be her doctor at this time. He had been one of her linguistic students at SIL in Grand Forks, North Dakota. With his parents in Chinese work in Manila, he had been interested in OMF. He and Hazel had long, interesting conversations as he gave Hazel transportation to conferences. Hazel in turn helped him stamp envelopes for his form letters. He finally did join the OMF family in the Philippines. Now from Manila Hazel wrote, "Our own Dr. Ed Glazier was helping out at the hospital for a while." Dr. Glazier always seemed to instill peace in Hazel's heart.

It would be several days before the results of the tests came back. So Hazel waited in Manila. She had language materials with her at the Mission Home and over ninety personal Christmas letters to answer. Throughout her life, "waiting" to Hazel meant a few minutes to read, write letters, pray or knit. Alban Douglas was also in Manila, and that meant discussions about stamp collecting. He had a collection of 6,054 stamps from 175 countries. Hazel determined to put her own stamp collection in order…"and count them and see how I stand in comparison to him."

What a relief when the tests revealed no sign of cancer. Hazel was soon on her way back to her field, loaded down with canned goods, books, and other supplies, plus iron pills. One of the books she carried was a precious new Tagalog book, *48 Lessons For Children*. It would make good reading on the five-hour trip to Mansalay.

Furlough was again on the horizon for Hazel, so once more she was pushing to get translation work finished and certain doctrines taught before she left. Word came that her mother was very low, and Hazel felt pulled in different directions. If her mother needed her, she would go home, but there was so much to do here on the mission field. She prayed about it, and the Lord answered prayer. Her mother began to regain her strength.

If she could only teach some of the people to read, they could read the Word to others while she was away. Hazel went to a little village about a half-hour's walk from Binli. Two men knew the alphabet and were able to read slowly with few mistakes. After only two weeks of reading lessons, they were put to work on Sunday, each reading a Bible verse. This was quite an accomplishment. These new readers were also able to check for errors as the girls did translation work. This was very important. They still had difficulty translating certain key words like peace, glory and flesh, but the Holy Spirit always led them to the right words. Hazel would translate difficult places in the Gospel of Mark ahead of time, leaving the final work to be done with Usig's help, sometimes working late into the evening.

There was a problem. Ann and Hazel were scheduled to leave on furlough at the same time. Unless another worker arrived for the Hanunoo work, Elly would be alone for a long time. Then Ann asked to delay her furlough, so that she could go at the same time as the Reeds (Mrs. Reed was her sister). If Hazel could leave in November, a few months earlier than planned, Elly would be alone for only a short time. The leadership in Singapore agreed to this. Suddenly, Hazel had only months left to complete all the things she wanted done. She finished copying the words into her English-Hanunoo Dictionary, 6,968 words in all. She wished she knew them all! Hazel busied herself working on the verbs and found them fascinating and gradually becoming clearer.

The last day of July three women and one man were baptised in the Sinariri River. Hazel spoke on "Separation unto the Lord." Good! Every baptism was an evidence of spiritual growth among the Christians. The tribal conference was just ahead, and Hazel prepared with great excitement. It was being held in her old territory. Daphne travelled with her, and they were near enough to visit Ayan Bukug and Bayanan. In Ayan Bukug they were welcomed with joy, and Hazel used every Alangan word she could remember. In Kaagutayan, Anghel and Rosario came from their fields at dusk to visit them.

The Sunday morning service, all in the Iraya language, was pure joy to Hazel's heart. Even the Scriptures read in Tagalog, were explained in Iraya by Anghel. After Hazel's message, Anghel gave an hour's sermon in Iraya on Luke 19. Spiritual growth was so obvious in the lives of many of the believers. Anghel had continued on with translation work and had written a tract entitled "The Way of Life." His dream was to have the entire Bible in Iraya. Hazel shared his dream!

In September of 1961, it was Ann's turn for medical tests to see what was causing the pain in her side. Surgery was performed to remove a lump. Back in Binli, Usig stayed home from his fieldwork several days so they could complete the first rough draft of the Gospel of Mark in Hanunoo. A few spaces had to be left where they hadn't yet found the right words, but they finished the translation on October 16. The next day Usig began to harvest his rice crop. Hazel wrote, "I am sure God is blessing him for putting first things first. Usig has grown in grace and in the knowledge of the Lord through the translation work. He is preaching with more confidence and even does some translation work on his own when we are not here." The Gospel of Mark would be the study book for one of the classes this year for the Short Term Bible School to be held at Sinariri. With more than twenty-five readers among the believers now, they added a class on how to study the Bible for themselves. This time leaving for furlough was not quite so traumatic. Some of the people could read the Word, and more of the Word was available to them.

Hazel left for her furlough with ten pieces of luggage. That included six broken phonographs and two typewriters for her to leave in Manila for repair. Phonographs were so vital to the spiritual growth of the believers. If they could be repaired and returned, that, too, might prevent some from falling back into their old ways.

By the end of November 1961, Hazel was in Canada. She was looking forward to presenting the work in the Philippines. Along with her own slides and literature, she had with her the film, "Love Outpoured." It included the story of Grandma Flower, who lived in a shack next door to Hazel in Bayanan. Grandma Flower's story was amazing. When she was young, a Filipino boy had come up to the hills and told of the Saviour he had found. It made a great impact on her as a young girl. The boy returned home, was beaten and never allowed to return. For fifty years Grandma Flower never forgot what she had heard. When Hazel arrived with the *Good News of the Gospel,* Grandma Flower's wizened face glowed. "Those are the words I heard fifty years ago." Grandma Flower (Bulaklak) became a keen believer, who thought nothing of limping ten hours back into the interior to tell her relatives about Jesus. Many came to know the Saviour through her life and her death. She fell crossing a hanging bridge of bamboo and vines and was killed on the rocks below. Her story epitomised what the Lord was doing.

This time when Hazel went across Canada, she took her parents with her. They visited Vi's sons, Rodney and Richard, in Saskatoon. Thinking it would be fun to see their old neighbourhood, Hazel and her parents rode out there in the evening on the Mayfair bus. After all these years, was it possible the Yoos family would still be there? They decided to find out, and what a reunion they had with their old friends. Mr. Yoos drove them to the train later, and they were on their way to Toronto. Prayer conferences were already lined up for Hazel at Gananoque and Orillia, Ontario. Her parents visited with relatives in the area and then went back home, while Hazel travelled on to New Brunswick and Nova Scotia.

All the missionaries, Hazel included, were shocked when they learned that OMF missionary Roy Orpin, in North Thailand, had been shot and killed. He had been married only a year, and his wife was in Manorom Hospital for the birth of their first baby. Hazel's heart couldn't have been heavier if it had been one of her own blood relatives. She felt an even greater challenge to urge the churches to pray.

Hazel's visit to Andover, New Brunswick, was very special. The Sunday school children in Andover had donated some of the tape recorders Hazel used in the Philippines. Now they would meet the missionary and hear real stories of how their gifts were reaching people for Christ. The pastor requested also that Hazel explain certain things she didn't usually include in her talks. At both of his two preaching points, Hazel spoke well over her time limit. After she had come all that way, the pastor stated, he wasn't going to cut her time short!

Hazel visited relatives, went to Hamilton and London, Ontario, and then went south into the United States. She visited Buffalo, Detroit, Lansing, Chicago, Wheaton and Minneapolis, and all along the way she met, visited, or phoned friends.

Her message to the churches changed again when a letter caught up with her from Dr. Broomhall. She would not be going back to the Hanunoo, but to the Iraya on the west of the island. Hazel was thrilled! The Mission had decided to let her work on translation for the Iraya and she would be working alone. She accepted! "That will mean I can work ahead at my own speed and not bother anyone. They suggested that maybe after a couple of years I will have enough translation work done so I can go back to the Hanunoo work." Hazel's own speed was usually much faster than anyone else could handle!

Hazel had covered fifteen thousand miles in eight provinces and seven states during this furlough, but one more adventure awaited her before she left. While visiting the Multnomah School of the Bible in Portland, OR, Hazel was interviewed in an anthropology class. Her type of work with the tribal people of Mindoro was the dream of these students. Some of them stopped to chat afterwards, and Hazel prayed that some day she would see some of these young people in the Philippines.

This time before she went back to the Philippines, she and her parents cleaned the attic. Hazel didn't want to leave again with that guilt on her mind. They found old pictures of her grandparents and of her parents with Vi and Florence. After the attic was done, they put family photos in the album. Then she was on her way again in November 1962, after a year at home.

She was happy to be working in the Iraya language again, but this time she was on the west side of the island, Occidental Mindoro. Dorothy Reiber was her guide on the one and a half hour hike from Mamburao to Kalamintao. Their first job was finding the Mayor. They finally found his wife. She was delighted at Hazel's attempt to say a few things in Iraya. Tomas, the mayor, had gone as far as grade seven in school with an eighty-five-percent average. He spoke English quite easily and was keen on helping with translation. What an answer to prayer! What was even more exciting to Hazel was that Tomas wanted to have a conference with people from all three Iraya dialects. He figured that if they all helped with translating, they could choose words known to all three groups. Anghel was his cousin, but spoke a different dialect.

Hazel wanted to be where she would hear Iraya all the time, but Tomas didn't think it was wise. The people moved so often that at times no one would know where she was. But it was the best way for her to learn more of the language. Finally Tomas found a place he thought would suit her, in Dikoy's village. Tomas explained to Dikoy that they need not fear Hazel, even though she was big and white and wore clothes. Dikoy seemed nervous about how the people would receive her. None of the adults welcomed Hazel. Not one person asked her to stay in their home. Finally, Dikoy's son made her a shelter for the night, a platform with a slanting roof covered with branches. The people themselves didn't even have blankets but kept warm by the fire at night. All of them, women and men, wore loincloths.

Hazel knew that working alongside the people was the best way to get to know them, so for nine days she helped the women gather wood and carry water. She helped them with their main food—the poisonous nami, which takes two or three days to prepare. All the time she was hearing, and using, the language. They wondered why she was there. Some suspected she was looking for a Mangyan husband. Hazel had only one purpose, to tell them of Christ, and they did seem interested as they listened to the records.

Hazel was sleeping soundly late one night when suddenly the silence of the dark jungle was filled with angry shouting. Hazel understood what they were saying. The elder of the group had returned home. He was angry to find that Hazel was in their village and he was threatening to rape her. Would this be a repeat of her horrible experience in Mexico? She was powerless to do anything but pray.

# CHAPTER 16

## TO THE IRAYA

The Lord heard her cry for help, and the jungle became quiet again. She did sleep, but early in the morning, before breakfast, Dikoy rushed her out of the village and back to Mayor Tomas. That was fine. Hazel preferred to live where she was wanted.

The people of Tikes Malalem did want her to live with them. They made a house for her and even helped bring her things from Kalamintao. Was this the place the Lord had prepared for her? Daphne and Mary Jane had visited here in the past, leaving a phonograph and records. The people had been schooled and could read the Tagalog Scripture. They knew some songs and Bible verses. Hazel could build on that foundation, and these people were keen to learn.

Hazel listened to the people and wrote down their words. Her Iraya dictionary was growing fast. She also made sure she spent time with the people in fun and work, each day. She learned different words at those times. One day she joined four women who were washing their *nami*, a poisonous tuber that had to be peeled, sliced and soaked for several days in a special bark trough to draw out the poison. Then it was washed and was edible. Hazel heard more new words, but she didn't have any paper to write them on. Being a creative person, she wrote them on the white cloth cover of her pail. The women were amused at that. Another day, as the ladies were bathing, Hazel scrubbed a woman's back for her. Little by little she was winning their trust. She wasn't surprised when five women prayed, confessing sin and professing faith in Christ. Hazel was not absolutely sure this was the group she should live with for the rainy season. She had not visited Kasagi and other places in this area yet.

Even though the Translators' Institute took Hazel away from the people, it was a positive experience, where she learned new methods to make translation easier and faster. In April 1963, she joined over seventy translators at Faith Academy outside of Manila for in-depth instruction. As the *Rules and Principles of Translation* were presented, they made sense to Hazel and would apply to any language. They heard the different meanings for the word *Spirit* as it appears in both Old and New Testaments, and another class taught them to break these down into even the right shade of meaning. But of special interest to her was the study of key words that gave trouble in every translation. Hazel's next big job was to pass these teachings on to her tribal translation helpers.

Anghel had been a great help when Hazel and Frances first worked with the Iraya people. Now she was pleased to be back with the Iraya and working with him again, as well as his wife, Rosario. They finished checking the first five chapters of the Gospel of Mark. These were then revised and re-typed, ready to go to Manila to be duplicated.

Tragedy struck their mission family again. Two Mindoro missionaries were killed in an accident. May Roy from New Zealand was one of their few Iraya missionaries. She had served in India, then China, and for the past ten years in the Philippines. Nessie Bell of Ireland had joined the Philippine group only a year earlier. They would be greatly missed, as both friends and co-workers. The third person in the vehicle, Ruth Fahrni, had been married only weeks earlier. She was thrown clear and survived. At a time like this, other missionaries couldn't help but consider their own vulnerability. Hazel wrote to her father asking advice about her own Last Will and Testament, but added, "Don't feel sad about the above subject—it is a routine thing for missionaries and 'our times are in His hands.'" If she died, the Mission would give her family a list of her possessions, and they could take what they wanted.

Hazel was a bit surprised to meet a Hanunoo prisoner in Mamburo one day. He was working on a nearby house, so Hazel stopped to chat and perhaps share the Gospel with him. As they talked, two Iraya prisoners from Kalamintao arrived. They were getting a great laugh out of the Hanunoo conversation when Hazel suddenly turned and talked to them in Iraya. She almost chuckled out loud at their surprise, and especially when they changed to Tagalog to be understood. The Hanunoo prisoner remarked that missionaries have power with God and asked for prayer for himself. He wanted more to read in the Hanunoo script, so Hazel wrote out some of the Gospel of Mark for him.

One person, who was an inspiration and joy to all the missionaries, was blind Huaning, living with the consequences of his past. Lime, extracted from snail shells, was used to make their addictive betel nut/tobacco combination. Obtaining lime was a long, sometimes dangerous, procedure. The shells would be tied in a large leaf and placed in red-hot coals. When the bundle was carefully opened, the shells would be white hot. Immediately, cold water would be dashed on them. When Huaning was young the water hitting the hot shells sputtered and bits of lime flew into his eyes. He had been blind ever since.

One day his wife learned about Jesus and placed her trust in Him. When missionaries came to his home to study the Word with his wife, Huaning listened. The Lord's love reached out to him, and he too gave his life to the Lord. Since then, he shared the news of salvation with everyone he met. This habit of chewing betel nut and tobacco, and the constant spitting, was a messy business. It was an addictive habit that most Christians shunned. But at times when tribal people tried to spit out of Hazel's plastic-covered window it was downright hilarious.

Daphne Parker was assigned to work with Hazel in this area. Daphne and Mary Jane (now Mary Jane Thompson) had been the first missionaries to bring the Gospel to these people. Hazel was thrilled to have an experienced co-worker. The Iraya in Kasagi prepared a house for Daphne and Hazel and invited them to live there for the rainy season. That suited them. Kasagi was central, and from that area they could easily visit the other places. This was the place the Lord had prepared for them.

One day Hazel overheard the Kasagi people talk about a group of tribal people she had never heard about. They lived in the interior, had no bad habits, didn't speak against their neighbours, or take other men's wives. They sounded almost perfect. Then she heard the other side of the story. Their one bad habit was stealing. Hazel was stunned to hear how they judged a suspect. First they would heat a piece of metal red-hot. Then the accused, to prove their innocence, was made to grasp the metal. Getting burned meant they were guilty. Hazel's heart ached to hear of beliefs like this. These people needed to know Christ, Who could give them victory over these superstitions.

When the busy Christmas Season arrived again, they shared the ancient story of Christ's birth in as many places as they could. Hazel had been working on the translation for the reading primer and after Christmas she set a goal. If she could have the primer done and stencils cut by the time she went to Baguio she could drop them off on her way. Perhaps she could pick them up coming back. This holiday she had five thousand stamps from one hundred countries to tell Alban Douglas about, and four missionary biographies to read.

"The persistent questions, which have been voiced for years as to whether there is a 'true' Iraya language and where it can be found, are still being heard," Cyril Weller's letter of March 15, stated. "At the last Field Council meeting it was recommended that a thorough linguistic survey be completed and a report prepared providing linguistic evidence which would clarify the issue. And, if possible, remove any further question of … spending time and talent on translating Scripture into the Iraya language…." Hazel had seen the advances being made in the Hanunoo, Buhid and Alangan languages. Would they finally be able to prioritise the Iraya language, too?

Hazel immediately wrote home asking for prayer. "The proposed survey is very welcome from my viewpoint. We don't know when they plan the survey or who is to do it, but these things are very important. The rainy season will be upon us after the conference in May and it would seem that the next two months it (the survey) should be done. I am also convinced that unless I can be on the survey team the picture may not be complete. If someone who speaks only Tagalog approaches the Iraya, they answer in Tagalog (it's the polite thing to do) but if you speak to them in Iraya, that is the language they use and even the women join in the conversation. Please pray that the Lord will lead in every detail of the matter and they may have the complete picture of the Iraya tribal situation."

Hazel was not responding in pride. She was stating a fact. Someone who knew both languages must be a part of the survey. Her prayers were answered. The Field Council finally sent word that they wanted Hazel and Daphne to do the survey before starting translation work in the Kasagi dialect. There were distinct instructions on what they were to look for. Hazel was ready to go but first Tomas took them high up in the fields where the people had never seen a white person before.

"These people must not have any blood, and that's why they're so white."

"Their noses are like ladders!"

These were the statements voiced by the tribal people. If they didn't have any blood, did that mean they were ghosts? The people were afraid of Hazel and Daphne. They hadn't even started on their fact-finding mission, but this trip was good preparation for what might be encountered.

Hazel and Daphne set out with a change of clothing, bedding, a tape recorder, Hazel's Iraya-English and English-Iraya dictionaries, dried fruit, Christmas cake, and some dried meat as snacks. They had the information collected in 1958 by Hazel and Betty Paeth. Plus they had the facts they had gathered the previous year in Western Mindoro. Were there really different dialects of the one language? How far is the Kaagutayan dialect (the one Anghel was translating) understood and used? Which dialect should they use for the basic translation, so that the whole Iraya group could use it? They had six days of mountainous jungle travel in Oriental Mindoro, a few days of rest, and three more days in Occidental Mindoro. In each place the people were glad to hear the message of salvation.

People in Oriental Mindoro were using Tagalog more than when Hazel had been there six years earlier. In Occidental Mindoro the people still preferred Iraya, and there were vast areas in the interior untouched. The Iraya people in the interior, from Mamburao south to Kasagi, needed teaching in their own language. That was their final answer!

While the missionaries were away, tragedy struck in Tikes Malalem. A young woman started to cough up blood one night and by morning both she and her unborn baby were dead. Fear swept in and the people were turning back to their old familiar customs. Rumours were flying everywhere: The spirits had punished her. Maybe her husband was not the father of the child. It happened because she had eaten her supper that night, in the dark! Then another woman died. Both women had professed Christ as Saviour. That was a blow to Hazel and Daphne. How could these people grow and live for the Lord, when they had no Bible to read for themselves? What the missionaries could teach them from visit to visit was not enough.

Hazel was one of four elected to the Field Council at their 1964 conference. This group met with the two superintendents to discuss the work in the Philippines, assign

133

people in the various areas, and keep up to date on what policies were needed. It was also announced at the conference that Hazel and Daphne would be doing Iraya tribal work on a permanent basis. Praise the Lord! Finally! Hazel would not have to rush through translation work before she was called somewhere else. Now they hoped to see a living church begun and growing. As Linguistic Examiner, Hazel would still get to visit the other areas when the missionaries took their tests. What could be better?

It had been fifteen years since Hazel had used her midwifery training. She was a bit surprised when a lowlander came for her help. His wife was in labour. The baby boy she helped deliver was fine, but around the ring finger of his left hand was a band of skin, not attached at all. Hazel asked permission to cut it off and also prayed with the mother and gave her a Gospel of John. The Lord certainly used interesting ways to get His Word out!

Another delivery made an even greater impact on Hazel's life. This was the delivery of a reconditioned blue Jeep, bought in Manila with special gifts from Central Baptist Church in Victoria. It would be used jointly by several missionaries in the area. Hazel and Daphne were suddenly taking driving lessons. This included driving not only on the roads, but also on narrow little bridges and through mud holes. It was time-consuming. Hazel didn't mind, because the end result would take hours off their travel time. Now they could visit their three points weekly and perhaps even answer some of the invitations from unreached places.

The year had been hard for Daphne, with little privacy, constant company, and exhausting trekking. When she was hit with the flu, she was hit hard. The doctor finally suggested that she should go to Baguio for a couple of weeks to recuperate, or longer if necessary. She left in November.

This year, at 6:00 A.M. on Christmas Day, the people in Kasagi began bringing gifts for the Lord. Hazel was pleased to see this spiritual growth. Before the Gospel arrived, the men would go to town at Christmas and ask for things from the Tagalogs, often coming home drunk. Now, they were giving to the Lord. The total of food and cash they brought was enough to buy nails for a new church building. The site had been chosen. What a change Christ had made.

More than seventy people heard the Christmas message, were treated to some candies, and received their cholera injections that day. It was the most convenient time to give injections, since many people seldom left their isolated homes. Hazel was almost moved to tears when one of the women stated that she didn't want Hazel to leave until her baby was more than two years old. She had already lost five children. "This woman is trusting in the Lord, and always comes to Sunday services," Hazel wrote home. "You can't blame them for wanting medical help."

Then it was time for Hazel to take her driver's test. Passing was vital so she could use the jeep and expand the ministry. She answered the twenty-five written questions and passed. Then she took the driving test. This was a little more difficult for her, but the Lord helped her. She got her license plus a bit of advice from the instructor. She needed more practice before driving in cities! Hazel smiled inside. She did not plan to do any city driving, ever!

Now that they could have weekly meetings in the villages, attendance increased. Interest in the Word flourished, and a good number turned from their fear of spirits to trust in the Living God, but Hazel was still not able to spend much time on translation work. Anghel continued working on a revision of the Gospel of Mark. Daphne was still not well. Towards the end of February, the doctor decided that Daphne wasn't strong enough for tribal life. Hazel was disappointed. Daphne had shared her keen interest in the Iraya people.

There were wonderful things happening, though. The people were preparing to build a new house for the Lord in Kasagi. A generous gift of money came for building the new church, and that presented another problem for Hazel to sort out. Money wasn't an issue, as the materials were already available. Getting people motivated to do the work was the greatest need. Hazel was very conscientious about using funds where they were designated. She needed to make some wise choices. The Lord again gave her wisdom. They would use the donated money to buy rice, salt, and fish paste to feed those who were working on the building. Suddenly the work was progressing much faster.

When Hazel went back to the Hanunoo area to give language examinations, she was surprised to find it hard to speak Hanunoo again. Gradually it came back to her. Hazel was so glad to see the Hanunoo hymnbook and translations of Scripture being used. Some of the people could read and sing quite well. After typing up material to leave for Ann's next examination, Hazel flew back to Mamburao. Again she was surprised. Less then an hour earlier she was thinking and speaking Hanunoo and suddenly she found she couldn't speak in Iraya. She had to revert to Tagalog for a while. By evening, after hearing the Iraya language all day, it was coming easier. On that day alone she had spoken four different languages. No wonder Wycliffe Bible Translators was asking her again to help at Summer Institutes of Linguistics on her next furlough.

The new OMF furlough manual now stated that missionaries were expected to be ready to take deputation meetings two months from the time they left the field. This made a big difference in Hazel's travel plans. It was much cheaper to go by boat, but that was a three-week trip. The financial aspect of going by boat appealed to Hazel's frugal nature. She could fly home in three days and spend the extra time with her parents. Choices! Always lots of choices to make, but she had a few months to decide.

Ten years had passed since Hazel and Morven Brown went to live at Ayan Bukug. The tenth anniversary celebration was one Hazel didn't want to miss! Ten years had brought about many wonderful and amazing changes.

Morven had translated Mark and Acts into Alangan, as well as hymns and Old Testament Bible stories. The believers had a great missionary vision, and as a result, there were baptised believers in at least three other places. This was also the Centennial Year of The China Inland Mission (now OMF). The tribal young people from the area presented a five-act drama, depicting the life of Hudson Taylor (founder of the mission). They had learned about him in their Short Term Bible School. What a fitting tribute to his life of dedication!

The Jeep saved a lot of travelling time, and made it possible to do twice as much. For instance, this August there would be four Short Term Bible Schools. Each village church where Hazel worked would host one. Of course, with the blessing of having a vehicle, came also the problems of upkeep, not an easy task for Hazel, who knew next to nothing about vehicles. Sometimes they would be stranded by a typhoon, because the river crossings were too deep to drive through. Then there was the problem of keeping the battery charged. Sometimes when the Jeep was in good shape, the roads were not fit for travel, so they were back to walking.

Hazel was never without things to do in the various villages. She made mix and match games for the children with printed syllable cards. The children loved them and didn't even realise they were being prepared to read Scriptures eventually. She made jigsaw puzzles out of cardboard pictures. Masiya was one of the young boys who was learning to read and had so much potential. At one time he had such a problem with fits of anger that his mother came to Hazel for prayer. Hazel prayed for him, and the next day Masiya came himself to visit Hazel. That day Masiya gave his heart to the Lord. Later he told Hazel, "A demon would enter my head, and I couldn't help but be angry. But the Lord has not allowed the demon to enter my head again." Hazel was right about his potential. Masiya was soon helping with translation.

The Lord always placed Hazel in the right place, at the right time. When she was asked to spend some time with

Mary Jane Thompson at Santa Cruz until Mary Jane's new co-worker arrived, the timing was perfect. Hazel needed the time to make another copy of her Iraya language file. This would be kept in Calapan in case of fire or some other calamity. When she had finished that, she went to Manila to check out a bit of "tummy trouble," as she often called it. Dr. Glazier found she had worms and gave her medicine to take care of the various internal visitors. Hazel was surprised when he also gave her a huge supply of UNICEF medicine for the tribal people. That flight home etched itself in Hazel's mind. Flames and red-hot lava spewed from the volcano at Taal. Entire towns were burned, and thousands of people died. How many of these people had died without ever hearing about Jesus Christ? The very thought spurred her on to work harder.

Hazel's prayer partners received the following review from the OMF in October of 1965: "We work among six of the seven Mangyan tribal groups (Iraya, Alangan, Tadyawan, Batangan, Buhid, Hanunoo and Ratagnon)." To the Filipino coastal people, all tribal people in the interior are called Mangyan. Each tribe has its own language and customs, and, sometimes, different names.

"Most of the people have only one change of clothing and blankets," the article continued. "They also have no place to keep things safely. Sometimes they roll a new garment in a large leaf and put it in an inconspicuous place between the grass shingles. If a friend or relative comes to visit they are almost sure to demand to see what is in the leaf ... if the visitor asks for it, it is hard for them to refuse. So people usually keep everything in a basket they carry with them. On Sunday the ladies wear the new dress or flour sack over the old one because if they left even the old one at home people could come in and help themselves (unbelievers who didn't attend church)."

Hazel had firsthand experience with this way of thinking. Her new khaki-coloured hand towel was hanging in her house. Visitors kept looking at it, and finally one of them asked for it. They thought that she must have had that towel for a long time for it to be such a colour. Hazel explained that it was new and the only one she had there. She wasn't sure that they believed the *new* part, since all of their belongings eventually end up that colour.

One day two men from the interior came to ask for a phonograph. Hazel was always glad to send out another of these "portable missionaries," but she didn't have one on hand. In eighteen days, she told them, she would bring one from Kasagi. The men immediately took a piece of cord and tied eighteen knots in it. Each day they would cut one knot off. When the last knot was gone, they would come to get the phonograph. These men listened well as she told them the story of Jesus for the first time. Times like this were wonderful for checking out dialects. She continued to translate between teaching and giving out medicines, but which dialect would be used still hadn't been determined. The STBS at Kalamintao would be a good testing ground for the translation work.

In November 1965, a tiny premature baby girl was born. Hazel called her Florence, since she was born on her sister Florence's birthday. For ten days the mother was too sick to care for the baby, so Hazel took care of her. This was nothing like being a midwife at Bethany Hospital. Here she had to carry water, wash diapers, cook, and clean, all with little help. When the mother died, family members took the baby.

"Through the caring for this wee helpless baby I came to realise more what it meant for the Almighty God to come to earth as a wee baby and limit Himself to all the helplessness of mankind so that He might become my Saviour and Lord."

Hazel visited the village of the baby's aunt some time later, only to find the baby alone, sucking on a bottle of sour milk, and with only a dirty rag around her. The aunt was in the next hut sick. The young girl who was supposed to look after the baby had gone away and left the baby alone all night. Something had to be done. The baby's father finally asked Hazel to take the child to her grandparents, Tibo and Ingga. Later, Elias and Lucing adopted the baby. Elias was in charge of the medical work in the area, and they were a wonderful family. Florence always had a special place in Hazel's heart. Whenever she visited them, Elias and Lucing would invite her to stay in a little room off their house.

One would think that the ultimate co-worker for any missionary would be one of the tribal people. So Hazel was quite interested when Inchang wanted to quit her job to become Hazel's helper. She could fish, hunt for food, prepare *nami*, and help with housework and translation. Inchang, a widow, had been working in the dormitory at Kalamintao, but the matron was not kind to her. Many people had been praying that Hazel would have a partner in the work. Perhaps this was the Lord's answer. Mr. Weller, the Superintendent, agreed to let them try it after Hazel's furlough.

Hazel moved with the Kasagi group to a new location, but Mr. Weller was not happy with her being in that area. The STBS scheduled there didn't work out. Classes in the evenings were not well attended. Things just seemed to be going downhill. One positive thing was that Ingga, Tibo's wife, helped with translation work, and they almost finished the Gospel of Mark. There were a few places left where Ingga refused to discuss the difficulties. Hazel finally moved to Kalamintao but continued to visit Kasagi.

Before going on her annual holiday, Hazel visited the Tadyawan, Hanunoo, and Buhid tribal people to take oral exams with four of the tribal workers. The highlight of the visits was the conference at Sinariri. Believers from Binli and Tarubong came, and the testimonies were spontaneous and up-to-date. Mark and Acts had now been translated and were being used. Hazel felt encouraged to expect great things also from the translations in Iraya. On her holidays, she spent her time sewing and playing Scrabble. One of the dresses she made was to be worn to Mary Jane's wedding to Bill Dick.

Daphne was the bridesmaid. Hazel was pleased to see Daphne well and busy in the lowland work.

Something had been at work while she was away. White ants had been diligently destroying anything edible. The papers around the gospel records were well eaten. Hazel took everything out into the yard and the hens had a great time cleaning up the ants. "It is one way to reduce one's papers," Hazel wrote home. Only a few of her written papers were damaged, but it took her most of the next day to get things in order.

This time when Hazel went on furlough, at least seventy records were at work, as well as every phonette she had on hand. The Lord was also preparing a wonderful illustration of His love and faithfulness for Hazel to share with the people in North America. One day on her way home, Hazel stopped at a stream to clean her teeth. Three hours earlier it had been a nicely filled stream, but now it was almost dry. She walked upstream, found a deeper spot, and cleaned her teeth. As she went downstream again, suddenly the shallow water was alive with shrimp flipping around. Some were quite a good size. Hazel began catching them and had twenty in a plastic bag when the stream started to fill up again. That day, the Lord blessed her with a lovely shrimp and banana salad for supper.

# CHAPTER 17

## ACCIDENTS AND DEATH

The Mission did not make decisions in haste. Sometimes it could take weeks or even months for requests to be dealt with, and then even longer before the answer made its way to the tribal area. It had been a while since Inchang first offered to quit her job and work with Hazel, when the good news arrived. Hazel had permission to ask Inchang to join her in the work. It would be wonderful to have someone working with her, and to have a tribal woman was more than she had hoped for. Hazel returned to the village to give Inchang the good news, only to find a wedding in progress. Inchang was being married at that very moment. Not having heard yet about permission to work with Hazel, perhaps she felt it was the only way out of her frustrating job situation. Hazel was saddened to learn that Inchang's husband left her just days after they were married and Inchang returned to work at the dormitory.

Months later, Hazel responded to an emergency summons: "Inchang has fallen. Come quickly." She found a crowd gathered at the dormitory. Part of the kitchen, where Inchang worked, was built on an overhang that extended past the outside of the house. Inchang had been cleaning that area when suddenly the structure collapsed and Inchang fell to the rocks eight feet below, landing on her head. The next morning the left side of her face was swollen, and she was numb from the waist down. Hazel hurried out to Alakaak to ask Elias for advice. Inchang should be taken to Dr. Abeleda in Mamburao, or in local terms, carried in a rattan swing to the highway. From Mamburao, Inchang was transferred to the National Orthopedic Hospital in Manila. Hazel went with her. Inchang had an injury at the base of her skull that left her paralysed.

It was with a heavy heart that Hazel returned to translation work. In August she finished the translation of Mark and read it to some of the women. It would be the final check to see if they understood it. There were still places that were not absolutely clear. Hazel took the manuscript to Manila to Mr. Mundhenk of the Bible Society for help, and day after day they worked on the problem areas. Then a bizarre thing happened. Late in the afternoon Hazel stepped out of the office into the dark hall. Suddenly she was tumbling headfirst down the stairs. Excruciating pain shot through her right shoulder and her nose as she crashed into the wall. Her concern was for her foot, painfully twisted under her. X-rays showed no broken bones in her foot. It was bandaged, and she began working again. Hazel took the manuscript to Inchang at the hospital to check changes with her. How ironic that she and Inchang had both suffered serious falls.

It took that week and the next to type the new changes, proofread the entire book, deliver it to be mimeographed, and then proofread thirty-six stencils. When two hundred copies were delivered to Hazel at the Mission Home, the joy made it all worthwhile. What a milestone! It was a delight for Hazel to distribute these Iraya Scriptures to Kasagi and Kalamintao before she left on furlough. An entire gospel was in print.

Another huge problem had also been solved. A stipulation for baptism was that the believers be able to read the Word, to obtain spiritual food themselves. When there were no Scriptures in their language, it caused frustration on both sides. Hazel could now go on furlough with a light heart. Ignoring the constant pain in her shoulder, she moved belongings to Mambarao to be stored and then visited at

Alakaak before leaving. She was sorry that she would miss Florence's first birthday. The Jeep was taken to Pinamalayan to be used in the work there while she was gone.

Her furlough began with almost three months of physiotherapy and exercise to loosen the impacted fracture of her shoulder, the result of her fall in Manila. Hazel, as usual, gave the Lord praise for saving her from worse injury. This so impressed the physiotherapist that she did all of Hazel's treatments free. She attended her nephew, Raymond's, wedding in Vancouver, took her parents as far as Toronto when she went across Canada on tour, and for the first time in many years, their immediate family were all together in Saskatoon.

"Since the middle of February I have had ninety-five opportunities to tell of the work in the Philippines and show slides," Hazel wrote to her prayer partners. It had been a busy furlough so far, and her summer assignment with Wycliffe's SIL in Grand Forks, North Dakota, hadn't even started yet. Hazel was looking forward to this assignment. Marjorie Davis, from Mexico, was the head teacher of Phonetics, and it had been twenty-four years since Hazel was in Mexico. She soaked up all the news.

Back in the Philippines, missionaries were being assigned to new locations. Neville Cooper, OMF Superintendent, wrote to Hazel. Would she consider teaching at the Mangyan Bible School when she returned to the Philippines? The Bible School had been a natural outcome of the STBS and was meeting the need for trained national leaders. Hazel prayed, but she couldn't ignore the fact that the Lord had gifted her for translation work. Other people could teach. Not everyone could translate. After further correspondence, she was glad to learn that she would return to the Iraya language group and be based in Mamburao. Once again the focus of her mission presentation had changed mid-stream. It was always easier to present the work to supporters, new and old, when she knew what she would be doing. Her list of supporters continued to grow.

Hazel's return to the Philippines, in November 1967, was a bit comical. If she left Canada wearing a coat, it would just be an encumbrance once she boarded the plane. So instead, she left home dressed in layers: a summer skirt and blouse under a woollen skirt and a long-sleeved blouse, along with woolly pants and two sweaters. She had to chuckle as she remembered doing the same thing in China years earlier. By the time she arrived in Manila, she had taken off layers of clothing. Her bag was full, but she was comfortable. Hazel could hardly wait to get back to see her Iraya people, but first she had a visit to make. Florence was living in Manila with Lucing's mother and aunt. She politely said, "Thank you, Lola (Grandma)," in Tagalog when Hazel gave her the dress she had made for her. The little girl also spoke Ilocano. She was small but obviously healthy and much loved.

Back on the island of Mindoro, a bus took Hazel close to where Tibo and the Kasagi folks lived. Hazel was pleased to find the trail much improved, but when she got to her destination the village was gone. Vanished! Where would they have moved and why? Sometimes a whole village would move when the stench of human excrement became overpowering. How could she find them? As she looked around, she spotted houses set on a ridge. People began appearing at the edge of the trail and by the time she climbed the hill, a whole row of her beloved, dark-skinned tribal people waited to greet her. They were so excited to see her. Almost bursting with a secret they joyously led her to one side of the ridge. There stood a brand-new house. It was for her! Tibo had started building it as soon as he heard that Hazel had arrived in Manila. This was an answer to prayer, a great contrast to some of her past experiences with housing.

Hazel was glad to be back and had constant company. Even on washday at the river she had company. A little boy and girl joined her there and received a good soaping from head to toe with rose soap. It was a treat for them, and they were careful not to rinse their hair too thoroughly. Their sweet smelling heads were proof that they had been to the river with her. Hazel had a surprise, too, for

145

the children. She had dressed little dark-skinned dolls in native dress to use as curios on furlough. Now she offered them to the Kasagi children to play with. Their reaction was interesting. When they saw the realistic eyes, even the adults ran out of the house in fear. She explained that those were only toys, but still it took time for the people to understand. Hazel understood their fear, because evil spirits were such a huge part of their lives. Soon all but a few were playing with the dolls.

That day a girl, very thin and in great pain, came for medicine. She was wearing charms, believing they would chase away the evil spirits that were making her sick. When Hazel explained that God is all-powerful, and hates anything in which we trust instead of Him, the girl asked the Lord to forgive her. Taking off the charms, she threw them into the bushes behind Hazel's house. Hazel gave her medicine and she went home.

Later that day, thinking the girl might be tempted to come back for them, Hazel burned the charms along with her trash. Suddenly Hazel had a headache, then pains in her stomach. She lay on the floor of her house in agony. Finally she spread out her mat, hung her mosquito net and went to bed. As she lay there talking with the Lord, she realised that her pain was an attack of the evil one, because she had burned the charms. Just that morning she had read the verse, "With God all things are possible." Hazel prayed and claimed the blood of the Lord as her protection. Immediately the pain was gone and she went off to sleep.

After Christmas, Mr. Elizalde, his wife, and a group of doctors and nurses held a clinic in Kalamintao to help the seven hundred Mangyan who gathered there. Mr. Elizalde, a wealthy man, had a huge heart for the Mangyan people. He had provided a wheelchair and even a home for Inchang. Carlos was helping set up the clinic, carrying heavy boxes of medicine, when suddenly his TB-riddled lungs haemorrhaged. That night Hazel sat with him as the Dextrose dripped into his veins. He was given nine bottles of Dextrose before returning home. At the same time, word came from

Kasagi that Hobita, Tibo's daughter-in-law, was unconscious. Mr. Elizalde arranged for a boat to take Hobita, Carlos, and others to the hospital in Sablayan. The next afternoon Hobita died from tubercular meningitis. Tibo confessed his acceptance of the Lord the day of Hobita's funeral, and Carlos also came to know the Lord.

These physical needs of the people weighed heavily on Hazel's heart. One day on the bus Hazel saw a doctor from the Health Clinic. Hazel asked his advice about people in a different area who were sick, and he wrote out a slip for her to get UNICEF medicines at the clinic. Hazel was amazed at what they gave her. It was much more than was needed. When Hazel returned with a report to the clinic of how the medicines had been distributed, the nurse gave her medicine for other places she visited. Sometimes the medicine was too late.

In February Hazel had the uncomfortable job of helping to dig a grave. The girl who had given up her charms died quite suddenly. There was a lot of weeping at the funeral. Her mother was upset, not that her daughter had died, but that she had never received a "bride price" for her. Hazel was content to hear that the girl was not afraid to die.

Now Hazel began having problems with the Jeep. Even with a new battery it often wouldn't start. Finally, it was stranded at the Santa Cruz crossing, where the bridge was out. It was safely covered with plastic, and both the engine and gas tank were locked. Neville Cooper suggested that it be brought to Mamburao as soon as possible. A friend, who claimed to be a mechanic, helped Hazel push it through the water. When they realised they were low on gas, the friend did what he had done to other vehicles in a similar situation. He added water to the gas tank! Surprisingly, it worked fine until they got to Mamburao. By then it needed a complete overhaul.

Sometimes, though, the advice of friends was very helpful. Their wells at Kasagi and in town had been re-dug, so there was a good flow of water in each place, but a washer kept wearing out. Such a little thing, but it couldn't be bought off the shelf at the corner store. Hazel sewed the washer together four times to make it last longer. Then a Christian lowlander showed her how to make a washer out of a rubber slipper. Good advice!

By the end of March, Carlos was physically able to give regular help in the language, one hour in the morning with new words and phrases, and an hour in the afternoon with translation. This year the church building at Kasagi was finished and the grounds cleaned up for the Believers' Conference, and a nice group came from the Abra de Ilog and Paluan areas. All but one of the visitors could read and had their own Bibles and hymnbooks. That spurred some of the local believers to learn to read. Hazel was puzzled when the Kasagi folks didn't turn out in as great numbers as usual. It didn't take her long to discover why. The visitors all had nice clothes, and many of the Kasagi people felt that their clothes were not good enough, so they stayed home. As usual, Hazel turned this into a teaching moment.

Then there was the Bible Translators' Conference, Hazel's delight. The teachers were specialists, and every class applied to Hazel's work: Bible Translation Problems; How to Work on a Common-Language Translation; Theory and Practice; and Biblical Backgrounds. She soaked it up! Over one hundred attended, and in the afternoon they divided into groups to check individual translations. This year Hazel also took the opportunity to learn Hebrew. The first day there were thirty-five students in the class, the second day twenty-five, the third day only fifteen. Hazel had to study hard, but by the end of the three weeks she wrote, "We can now read the Old Testament in Hebrew and look up new words in a lexicon .... We should be helped in translating the Old Testament in days to come." She had vision, all right!

One day, Hazel's guides took her to a new village. The people, all of one family, had moved from Camurong the past March. Besides the father, Euhilyo, there were his five sons and three daughters. They had begun trusting the Lord less than a year earlier and were thirsty souls. Hazel was given a place to sleep in the church. Pasita, one of the daughters, slept there with her and cooked for them. The next morning more than twenty came to study the Word for a couple of hours. Felis, one of the sons who had studied for two months at the Mangyan Bible School, told her how glad they were to be taught in Iraya. Now they could go back to the fifty or so families where they used to live and give them the message. The sons, Felisiano (Felis), Amyano, Oding, Pasyo and Minis, had missionary hearts. The three girls, Pasita, Hulya and Talya, became vital parts of Hazel's ministry. Some of the next generation, Sisar, Milya, Iprim and Tito would be just as vibrant. Hazel was interested to find that five sets of twins were born into this family over the three generations she was acquainted with. Minis and Pasita were twins, and would eventually each have twins of their own.

Felisiano-translator

Pasita-translator

Six of the people could read and were willing to mark places in the translation where they had difficulty understanding the Iraya translation of Mark. The Lord prompted Hazel to go to Kaagutayan, where Anghel spent six hours that afternoon and the next morning reading the translation of Mark and giving suggestions for improvements.

From Kaagutayan, she tracked down the folks from Communal who had moved, and they seemed very glad to have the Iraya translation of Mark. She went on to Bayanan, and, being so close to Ayan Bukug, she then visited Morven Brown and other folks who were home.

Hazel was heartbroken to learn of the death of her oldest nephew, Philip, in a car accident in August. It was one of those times when it was hard to be so far from home. Philip, Vi's son, was only thirty-four years old. Hazel took comfort in the fact that he was a fine Christian. She wrote to her sister, "Truly Philip has been given to us of the Lord for these short thirty-four years and almost five months. He has been a blessing and joy to me and I'm sure to you also. We are sure the Lord will bring glory to His Name even through his death."

Only two months later, as Hazel was praying for her family, she found it strange that she couldn't find anything to pray about for her mother. She must be fine. When Neville Cooper arrived in the village, he was talking to Felis very quietly before Hazel realised he was there. She was not as surprised as she might have been when Neville told her that her mother had passed away on October 15, 1968. The next day Hazel went by bus, boat and jeepney to Mamburao. One of the Christians working in the government office was able to explain the situation, and within a few hours she had an exit permit and all the papers needed to re-enter the Philippines. She packed and made a quick trip to Kasagi to arrange for someone to look after her house and contents there. The next morning she flew to Manila. A special gift had already come in, enough to cover her whole return flight. Hazel later learned that this generous gift was from one of her former Sunday school students in Victoria.

Hazel arrived in Victoria a week after her mother had died, and missed her funeral. How strange to come home and not be met by her mother. Irvine and John had returned home, but Vi was still there and stayed for a few days. Hazel was glad that they could be there for their father, to grieve with him and talk over a lifetime of memories. Her father planned to stay on in the home for as long as he could care for himself. As Hazel thought about returning to the Philippines, she did not feel comfortable about leaving her father alone. She prayed fervently that the Lord would provide someone to live with him by the time she was scheduled to leave.

Hazel had first met Alberta Davis in 1941. She was one of the Canadian girls who went to China with Hazel in 1946. Alberta had looked after her own father several years earlier, and now she was willing to live in the house to cook, clean and care for Mr. Page. She would also find a full-time job in the area. Alberta was the answer to Hazel's prayers. She arrived at the end of November and was an immediate blessing. She drove Hazel and her father to the cemetery, then around to call on Mr. Page's cousin and sister. What a different, sombre Christmas this one was, without her mother, and knowing that two days later Hazel would also leave.

At least that was the plan! Victoria was inundated by a snowstorm, leaving the roads to the airport, several kilometres north of Victoria, next to impassable. Hazel and her Dad trudged through deep snow to where the airport limousine would pick them up. Hazel carried her 44-pound suitcase and her shoulder bag while her father carried her piece of hand luggage. They were very glad when two young men offered to help with the heavy case. The limo was an hour late, but with close to thirty passengers on board, they expected that the airplane would wait for them. It didn't. The airline changed her reservation to a flight two days later. Hazel left her suitcase at the airport. She and her father returned to Victoria in the limo, free of charge, and again struggled home through the snow.

When she finally arrived in Manila, it was to the news that the Davenports had a new baby boy, Joel, born the day

Hazel arrived. Then the Fullers had twins, Sharon and Stephen. Hazel visited Inchang and found her cheerful, but lonely. There was a pile of mail waiting for her when she arrived in Mamburao. She visited Kalamintao one day and then spent two weeks in Kasagi. Hazel was disappointed to see several children at Kasagi wearing charms again. "Probably in the absence of a good supply of medicine when I was away they turned back to their old ways of dealing with sicknesses." But with the Lord's help, they were learning. Otlo, the daughter-in-law of Tibo and Ingga, became delirious with a high fever. Remembering how their daughter-in-law, Hobita, had died the year before, Ingga left to get a man to drive out the evil spirits. Hazel quickly explained again that they must trust God. "Although Satan is powerful," she explained, "God is more powerful." They called Ingga back and Hazel led them in prayer, asking the Lord to defeat the power of Satan in Otlo, if this was his attack. She gave Otlo aspirin to take down the fever, but she was still unconscious when they arrived at the Mamburao Hospital the next morning. The doctor diagnosed her illness as cerebral malaria. It was treated and in a few days she was ready to return home.

The people had again seen the power of God, and over fifty people came out to the Sunday services. This was a step forward. These people desperately needed the Word of God, so that they could read these truths for themselves. One of their worship services ended with a wedding. The couple had been living together but had not married, even according to Iraya custom. They confessed their sin and made their marriage vows before the congregation and the Lord. Another step forward. She needed to take a small trunk of household and personal things to Kalamintao, so she could be there two weeks at a time.

Two of the Mangyan Bible School students, Sano and Sisar, stopped on their way to Talosian one day. Hazel had taught these boys in Ayan Bukug ten years earlier and was so pleased to see them going on with the Lord. Sano stayed and took the service, and Sisar went with Felis to help at

Kaagutayan. Then two girls made plans to go with Felis to teach God's Word to their relatives at Camurong and Odalo. Abelino contacted people at Tinganay and seventeen expressed an interest. In March when Hazel, Abelino and Felis went to visit these people, they welcomed Hazel and quickly prepared a simple shelter for her to use. They loaned her a pot for cooking rice and a coconut shell for a plate. One of the men made a wooden spoon for serving the hot rice and they shared their greens and snails and wild fruit with her. Hazel was not too keen on eating snails. "It takes so long to eat a meal with snails that when you're finished you can't decide if you are satisfied or not. But they are better than nothing."

Hazel was impressed with the eagerness of these people to study God's Word. Abelino and Felis taught about twenty-eight people every evening. Hazel spent her time teaching those most capable to learn to read. After three days' study, Benigno could recognise almost all the alphabet and read about half of the primer. One of the men who could read would continue to help Benigno and others. On Sunday thirty gathered for the service, and all of them indicated their desire to trust Christ as Saviour. Abelino had a field at Tinganay and planned to marry Felis' daughter, Rosing. Hazel rejoiced that the Lord was now raising up couples who could minister together. The Gospel spread most effectively in the Iraya tribe in this way, with people sharing the Gospel with their relatives. It was a wonderful natural contact.

Hazel preferred to spend weeks in these places rather than just visiting. "I am available when they have free time to study and there is no limit to the hours I teach. One has to be ready at a moment's notice. I never know until I hear the 'bell' (an old car spring) rung at the church." Hazel referred to this intense teaching time as "giving them a feast of the Word."

# CHAPTER 18

## LAND AGREEMENTS

Mine of Gold. *Mina de Oro* was the Spanish name for Mindoro, because there was gold in the mountains and rivers. All through Hazel's years in the Philippines, there were constant conflicts over land claim agreements. The Mangyan had lived on the land all their lives, but had no legal documents. People from other islands and from the lowlands came looking for wealth, wanting to move in and take over the land. Year after year, the tribal people moved farther and farther up the mountains, taking their children with them and planting their crops on the mountain slopes. The missionaries, along with Christian lawyers, negotiated with government agents and fought to obtain titles, legal documents, for these people who had farmed the land for decades. One man, claiming to be a land agent, tried several underhanded ways to obtain possession of the land. Christian lawyers discovered land agents had been done away with years earlier. He had no such rights.

Some things were improving for the people, though. The water supply in Kalamintao had undergone a radical change. Fifty men worked together to bring spring water near the village. Twenty-six bamboo tubes were fastened end to end to form a long pipe to channel this clean water to the people. It was an inventive idea, because holes at each joint allowed the water to flow out. The people could fill their containers or even bathe under its flow. Hazel saw, in this venture, a picture of the teamwork needed to bring the "Living Water" to those who hadn't heard the Gospel.

Hazel was seeing the "Living Water" flowing into new areas, and every place with the Gospel meant a need for regular Bible teaching. Hazel was eager to meet this need, but how could she possibly cover all these needs by herself? She began studies in new areas, Gisa and Gelgey, but being able to read the Word in their own language was still the only way these people could live victorious Christian lives. There was only one answer. The Lord would have to send more labourers into His harvest. Her prayer letters and personal letters reflected this.

Hazel's letters home to Victoria now were written to "Dad and Alberta," who were getting along fine. Hazel felt as if she had another sister, so it was no problem for her when her father decided to include Alberta in his will. He planned to leave his home jointly to Hazel and Alberta. Hazel was actually thrilled with this. It brought to Hazel's mind the thought that someday she and Alberta would retire in that home together. Hazel wrote to the lawyer, at her father's request, giving her consent.

"Dad has written to me recently asking me if I have written to you ... I want you to be assured that I am in full accord with having Miss Davis share the property with me. I know that there is no likelihood of Dad ever being without a home as long as Alberta and I live and have possession of the home. Since Dad prefers the transfer to be made while he is still with us, I believe we should comply with his request." With both names on the title and Alberta in residence, they could continue to receive the homeowner's grant. It would also save succession duties.

Some help for her on the field would be great, too. Someone else was praying about this. Shirley Charlton had been working in the Mission office for some time but really wanted to work with the tribal people. The Mission agreed that she could join Hazel in the Iraya work. Mr. Herren found them a house in San Teodoro. It would be ready by February

1970, when Shirley returned from her holiday to begin her study of Tagalog.

Seventy people came to the Christmas service in Kasagi, and their offering that day was seventeen pesos, almost as much as the total yearly offerings. Some of the money would be used to repair the church. The rest, they decided, would be used to help folks get to the Believers' Conference in Bayanan of Mayabig. Hazel encouraged as many as possible to go. She would go with them. On January 7, 1970, Hazel and seven Iraya Christians from Kasagi went by Jeep to Mamburao, and north to Abra de Ilog, where they joined Christians from three other villages. Even with the Christmas offering, they couldn't possibly afford to pay for transportation all the way, so wherever they could, they walked. Sand blew against their legs as they followed along the north coast of Mindoro and clambered over stretches of rocks in places where the waves were too close. They waded through several small rivers and were waist-deep in water crossing three larger rivers. That first day they reached Lukutan about 4:30 in the afternoon, and stopped there for the night. They slept in a loft.

The next leg of the trip was by boat from Puerto Galera to San Teodoro, then inland by bus to Alag. The last stretch was a muddy trek to Bayanan. The rivers had been impassable the day before, but now they were only waist deep. When they entered Bayanan, crowds of people were everywhere. Hazel was thrilled as she greeted believers from all six tribes in which OMF was working. Stories of what the Lord was doing in various areas encouraged the tribal Christians. Worship, fellowship, and teaching brought about spiritual growth and renewed vision to reach out to those around them.

Felis and his brothers were looking after the work in Gelgey and Gisa. They were not yet ready for Hazel to move there. She decided to go and worship with the people in Kaagutayan on Sunday. Tuesday morning she got the "GO" feeling. Gelgey was less than an hour away, and she felt an urgency to go to teach the people there for a few days. Around twenty people attended reading classes during the day and Bible study in the evening. Some of the men worked on a house for her. Why had she been drawn here at this time? She was about to leave when a man arrived with a list of thirty-seven people who were seeking the Lord in Talipanan near Puerto Galera. They were building a church, and a house for her to occupy as soon as she could come. She would begin to prepare, so that she would be ready when the people at Talipanan were ready for her.

First, she had to attend the Translators' Seminar, then she was scheduled for vacation (a mission requirement), and finally, the Tribal workshop. She would work in a week each at Kasagi, Liwliw and Kalamintao also. Sometimes she felt as if she was going in circles. Well, she was, going round and round to all the villages. How she longed for help! Always there was the pressing need to translate more books of the Bible for them. They didn't even have the entire New Testament in their own language.

"Approximately half of my time this past year has been spent in Oriental Mindoro," Hazel wrote in the Iraya *Station Report* for 1970, "and half in Occidental Mindoro amongst the Iraya groups who still use their own Iraya language. Both Gelgey and Gisa requested concentrated teaching and provided hospitality to make this possible. Togaaw has also extended the invitation for missionary teaching. At Talipanan thirty-seven have said they want to follow the Lord and receive missionary teaching. So, from now on, these five places will each receive a week's teaching in turn: Talosian, Togaaw, Gisa, Gelgey and Talipanan. All at Talosian who are of eligible age have been baptised. I plan to continue this cycle of teaching until there are enough trained leaders to carry on. Then I would like to settle down in one place and do translation work, providing materials for the leaders to use."

At the end of April, Hazel received a whole case of UNICEF free medicines. The plan was to give it out in three months, report on its distribution, and then get another case. There was medicine for infections, dysentery, itch, infected eyes, and more, plus vitamin and iron pills.

Another new location was the Igso group. Their new site required no river crossings from Mamburo, so she could visit even during the rainy season. They built a chapel with a raised floor at one end where Hazel could live, although she couldn't stand up in it. Dante and Castor were her guides on her first trip. Castor had been in her reading class a year earlier and had learned to read in only four or five days. It was a joy to see that he was still doing fine. Each morning she taught from Genesis, and each evening they studied Christian living. Hazel could describe their singing only as "making a joyful noise unto the Lord with all their hearts, bless them." No matter what tune Hazel was singing, everyone else sang the hymns to any tune.

Her visit at Kalamintao, the first in four months, was disappointing. These people had not been worshipping together when she wasn't there. God was obviously not first in their lives, and Hazel felt responsible. "I'm afraid I have failed to get the people to take part in the meetings enough when I am here so they don't do it when I'm not here." Thankfully, other places were more encouraging. Pancho, in Gelgey, could now use the references in his Bible and had memorised the names of the books of the New Testament, so that he could find Scripture passages quite quickly. It had been only a year since he made his stand for the Lord. Four families moved from their field houses to sleep in the village so they could study the Word mornings and evenings while Hazel was there.

Thirty from Togaaw attended the Believers' Conference and took Hazel back to Togaaw with them. This was a place where Felis and his brothers ministered, and Hazel felt very privileged to be the first missionary to live, or even visit, there. She lived in their municipal house with food and fuel provided. Under some of their houses were tiny wooden crosses. Hazel inquired about them, and a keen

Christian couple admitted that they were to scare away the demons. Hazel gave them some guidance from the Word in the evening service. These dear people had never been taught about other gods and were so glad to know God's will in this matter.

Hazel listed the names of families coming to the services. Names of people who had never attended were also mentioned, and then they prayed that those people would soon accept Christ as their Saviour. That very evening an entire family of eight came to the service for the first time, and all accepted Christ. The Christians were encouraged, especially the woman who had presented their names. An average of sixty came to study in the afternoon, and all ages were learning to read and write. Even more attended the worship service Sunday evening and listened well, especially when she spoke Iraya.

Who but Hazel would be the listening ear when people wanted to quote the memory verses they had memorised? Garito was one of the visitors who came to quote memory verses for her. The rest of his story thrilled her. Hazel had copied memory verses by hand for Cesar to memorise. Cesar, in turn, had used them to teach Garito. Here was Garito quoting them back to her. She rejoiced that the time spent copying the memory verses by hand had not been wasted.

Even giving injections could be turned into an opportunity to spread the Good News. Hazel scheduled time for folks to come for medication in the afternoon, and then invited them to stay for a filmstrip in the evening. One day as Hazel was giving injections, she had her own experience with a collapsing floor. No one was hurt, but Hazel had to pick up the thirty needles and a syringe off the ground and sterilise them all over again. The damage was soon repaired, and everyone enjoyed a filmstrip plus slides of themselves. Hazel did her best to prevent serious disease from attacking the villagers, but sometimes nothing could stop a devastating epidemic.

In December 1971, Hazel arrived at Kasagi to find the men digging a grave. A severe type of flu had hit the village, and the grave was for her dear friend and translation helper, Ingga, who had gone to be with the Lord. Hazel spoke from the Word and prayed with those at the graveside. Only two men in the entire village were strong enough to prepare food for all those who were sick. Hazel went from house to house, giving pills and liquids. In the late afternoon she repeated her round. The situation was serious. She needed help. It was a two-hour walk to catch the bus, but she had go and get advice from a doctor. He prescribed medication by injection, as well as vitamins and other pills. That afternoon Hazel injected thirty-three who were sick and gave vitamins and other pills to forty-seven more. The next morning those who could move gathered to worship. Then word came of similar sickness in the next valley. Hazel went there with medicine and was in time to save some lives.

Thankfully, there were some good things happening as well. There was rejoicing in February 1972, when the Kasagi land was finally released, and Tibo's lot was titled to him. The people were finally obtaining legal rights to their land.

Hazel's translation helpers had dwindled to Anghel in Kaagutayan, Pasita in Talosian, and Carlos in Kasagi. When Pasita went with Hazel to Kasagi, Hazel discovered that Carlos and Pasita made a good team. They discussed the dialect differences and made decisions concerning suitable words for the translation. When Carlos was too sick to help, his wife, Pakane, helped. Hazel was elated at the way that Pasita and Pakane freely discussed things. When Hazel was called to help others in the village, the women would continue on without her, writing down their translations to go over with Hazel later. One Sunday, Hazel wept with joy as twenty-year-old Pasita shared in the service how she had become a new creature in Christ. Everyone listened attentively to her.

Pasita was also proving to have a missionary heart. Not only was she teaching the people at Polapog, but she also

160

wanted to accompany Hazel on her trips to other villages. Hazel agreed to take her along on a trip to Occidental Mindoro. Together they got Pasita's clothes mended and ready to go. Pasita was an excellent helper, getting water, drying dishes, cooking. The two had Bible study together each day. At the end of the trip Pasita was willing to go with Hazel all the time, if it was the Lord's will and her family approved. Theo, the Field Chairman, consented for her to accompany Hazel two weeks every other month. This would give her time at home with her family and with her teaching at Polapog. She taught memory verses by rote, having the people repeat a verse ten times, and they learned the verses well.

Then Carlos offered to help pay Pasita's fare to go to Kasagi more often to translate. By February 15, 1972, they had finished the first draft of Philippians, and it was time to start preparing for furlough again. Hazel's vision was to have Philippians at least typed up for the Iraya believers to use while she was away. Revision, checking and publishing would have to wait until the next year. Looking back, she could see the progress that had been made from one furlough to the next.

Her possessions, scattered in all the various places she lived, had to be collected in one place. Then she packed, prepared language materials for Hermann and Doris Elsaesser for the coming year, got official papers for leaving, had dental work done (because it was much cheaper than in Canada), and lastly, attended the Tribal workshop. In all this activity she managed to take the newly translated Philippians to be mimeographed. It was done! One hundred copies of Philippians finished, to be used in the Iraya work while she was gone.

At home, Hazel missed her mother and saw big changes in her Dad. He had fallen and cracked his ribs the month before, but now he was well enough to go with Hazel on her cross-country tour. They spent more than a month in the Toronto area, while Hazel attended conferences in all directions. This time her father went with her all the way to St. John, New Brunswick. They toured Prince Edward Island. Then they went to Quebec City and visited Irvine's oldest son Wayne and his family, in Montreal. Her father was especially pleased to visit Elwin Perkins, who had been his hired man more than fifty years earlier.

It was evident that Mr. Page was not feeling well when they arrived back in Victoria. Hazel didn't think it was just exhaustion from the trip, so she phoned her brother John. They took their dad to the hospital and found he had an intestinal obstruction. A week or so later a malignant growth was removed. The doctors felt that it was localised, and by the third week in September he was home again and seemed fine. Hazel had mixed feelings as she thought about returning to the Philippines in January. As weeks passed, she realised that her father wasn't eating well and there were times when he was obviously in pain. By the middle of December her father had pain all through his abdomen. The growth had been active and spreading. There was nothing to be done now but to keep him comfortable. On December 19, 1972, after ten days in the hospital, he went home to be with the Lord.

Hazel had always been close to her father. They shared a love of gardening and could talk about anything. Everywhere she turned there were memories of him. Vi arrived from Saskatchewan and Hazel was glad that John lived so close and could help with decisions. He took over the responsibility of her father's will. There were sympathy cards to answer and heirlooms to be passed on. Hazel was especially glad to have Alberta's company. It was a different Christmas with both parents gone, and it was a different leave-taking. Alberta stayed on in the house.

Hazel mailed a letter to Vi from California on her way back to the Philippines. "I am enclosing a label off a jar of Grape conserve which Dad saved and wrote on. I found several such in Dad's pockets which showed that he thought of Mother each time a jar of jam was opened and rather cherished the label as a keepsake. Dear Dad."

Hazel was glad to be able to dive into the work and to keep busy. One of the highlights of 1973 was a month-long Translators' Institute. She wrote, "The emphasis has been on using the meaning given in the original Hebrew or Greek as we translate the Bible into the language on which we are working. In so many translations, even in English, there has been too much of a word-for-word equivalent translation or a tendency to translate the same Greek word as one English word – the same in every place. In every language there are different uses of the same word. For example: bought a chair; electric chair; address the chair; chair of philosophy. So in translation it would be silly to translate chair by the same word in each case."

Something new was added this year: the study of different types of literature, poetry, proverbs and riddles, and the purpose they fulfil in each language. The translators also studied the structure of a story or account, because each language has its own way of beginning paragraphs and sentences. Hazel was pleased that she had brought along a couple of stories so she could work out details with the expert help available. She had never done this kind of analysis before and would have to pass on what she learned to others working in translation with her. They also considered words that are hard to translate, such as grace, mercy, and peace. Hazel always found these discussions helpful.

When Margaret McKee, a friend from Victoria, arrived in August of that year, she was amazed at Hazel's stamina. Their day started before 4:00 A.M. and included hiking up leech-infested jungle paths to Kaagutayan and then on to Panalangdayan before dark. That was one day! Margaret watched tribal women flick insects into the fire to sizzle. She took part in an Iraya church service and taught them to sing a hymn. She met all the missionaries at an OMF prayer meeting. No doubt the focus of prayer on Hazel's behalf changed drastically when Margaret returned home.

163

For a long time, *Dicky* had been a part of Hazel's life. Now, early in 1974, she and Anghel spent long days working on the Iraya dictionary, or *Dicky*, as Hazel affectionately called it. She was pushing to get it done and in print. There were a thousand words that had not been entered yet, one-tenth of the vocabulary, so they could not be overlooked. Every word was needed. The more extensive the dictionary, the more apt they were to find words understood by all the dialects. The final dictionary would contain ten thousand entries as well as an index. This was all written by hand and then typed in Iraya, Tagalog and English. Hazel would have liked to work in the evening as well, but kerosene had become very expensive and hard to get. When her light was on at night, people would come to enjoy the light, so she didn't get any work done anyway.

Hazel's heart ached when she discovered that young Pasita was expecting a baby. The baby's father did not want to marry her. It was difficult to teach the unsaved about living for the Lord when the Christians themselves did not live victorious lives. Hazel delivered the baby girl, named Rebeka. It was a difficult delivery, and within months it was evident to Hazel that something was wrong with the child. Nine months later the baby was still not sitting up, although doctors could find nothing wrong. An older man with seven children wanted to marry Pasita, but she refused to marry any man other than Rebeka's father. Pasita and her baby stayed at home in Panalangdayan with her father, Euhilyo.

Hazel took her holiday this year at a lovely beach house near Iloilo. It belonged to the parents of Doctor Romeo Sanglap, who was from Iloilo but now lived and worked in Victoria. He and his extended family welcomed her as family and blessed her throughout the rest of her missionary career.

About this time Phil Holder began to talk to Hazel about a machine that could help finish the dictionary in a hurry. She was thrilled with the possibility that the job could be done quickly and well. Eric Parsons at Far East

Broadcasting Company tried out two pages of the dictionary and sent Hazel the results. She was amazed! The three indices were put in alphabetical order just with the push of a button. They made six copies: one for the files, two for the Elsaessers, two for the use of future Iraya language students, and one for her.

"Do you find words interesting? I do and it is a good job I do because I've been at the job of recording and analysing words for many years but during the last few weeks in a more concentrated fashion." Thus began a letter with an interesting review of some of Hazel's translation work. "For example, in Iraya there is a word 'lampas' with the basic meaning of 'going beyond'. If this takes a verbal form it speaks of people going back and forth past a certain point. When it is used as an adjective it means 'transparent'; the vision goes beyond a certain point. When it is used as a noun it means 'pride'; goes beyond what one should think of himself. I found this word very helpful but it is also confusing until you hear it in the right context. This is true with so many words even in English."

Hazel's prayer partners were always given lots of details, so that they could be praying effectively. One example concerned a workshop, which probably had only the usual difficulties. Everything had to be carried in. The water system was not working, so the water had to be carried up from the beach. Then the kerosene refrigerator was not working so ice was purchased and brought in to keep the milk from souring. Other notes in her letters told of the cost of electricity being four times as high as it was the previous year and of killing over five hundred snails in one day. Hazel was always thankful to have good prayer support.

# CHAPTER 19

## BROKEN LEGS

One day Felis arrived at Hazel's house with his son, Iprim, in a sling on his back, every step sending pain through the little boy's body. The children had been jumping off a porch to see who could jump the farthest. Iprim won the contest. But in winning he landed on a stick or stump. The result was a badly broken leg. As he lay in agony by the side of the trail waiting for his dad to come, Iprim asked his older sister, Rosing, to sing "The Great Physician." Hazel examined the break and explained their choices to Felis. They could set and splint the leg or carry him out to Calapan. Felis made splints. Hazel padded and covered them, and then they worked together to set the bone.

"It was a hard thing to see the boy suffer so much but I gave him a pill to kill the pain and he was brave. Felis held the leg at the buttocks and I pulled on the leg whenever Iprim said I could. He would say, 'Pull, Auntie, pull,' then, 'Stop, Auntie, stop.' Tears ran down his cheeks and down mine too." Hazel wrote. "But we kept on pulling and holding until the two legs were the same length." The splints were applied, and the adults shook hands and said, "Thank the Lord." Young Iprim extended his hands and smiled as he also praised God. Rosing stayed with him overnight at Hazel's house, but there wasn't much sleep.

"We had a praise service on Friday morning before I left, and prayed with our hands on Iprim's body. Felis prayed that those with broken spiritual legs might walk in the ways of the Lord and that Iprim might again walk and be able to carry God's Word to others."

Broken spiritual legs! Those who had never heard of the redeeming power of Christ. Some of these people Hazel had long wanted to reach lived at Langkaan, a hard day's trip from Kaagutayan, even for the tribal people. For years she had prayed for an opportunity. Finally she made the trip to Laagkaan (prologue). She was then fifty-eight years old. It was the first time a foreigner had ever been there. The water situation at Langkaan was not so good. The incline down to the water was steep and slippery, and the climb up was worse. Hazel went with two of the girls for water one day and could hardly manage it. The second time she put the water container in a pack on her back and found that easier. When she got home and weighed the load on her spring scales, it was nearly twenty-five pounds. No wonder it was hard to carry up the steep hill! The scale was one more thing Hazel used to determine details. She was pleased with the time of teaching there in Langkaan. The trip home was spiritually rewarding but physically gruelling.

"You may wonder where my bruises are," Hazel wrote to friends and family about her tumble down the mountainside. "One on the right shoulder blade, one at the right waist on the tummy, a big bruise on the right hip, one on the left thigh and one on the left calf. My neck muscles were also very tender but better now. Also at the base of the right breast there is a sore spot which throbs when I lie down and is painful if I cough or laugh. My legs were chapped raw from walking in wet clothes, but Watkins Medicated Ointment soon healed that up."

When they arrived back, even before looking after her own needs, Hazel accompanied Gabino and Ben to see the Police Commander to try to get a letter of protection for the Langkaan people. They were ready to flee higher into the safety of the mountains because of the pressure to send their children away to school. The Police Commander spoke to the principal of the Saclag School and said that they definitely would not force any child to go to Saclag against the parents' wishes. Hazel hoped Gabino would be happy with this. It would be sad to see the whole village move farther away, making it almost impossible to reach them.

Hazel received distressing news from Canada but in a roundabout way. Her brother John phoned Alberta. She, in turn, contacted Hazel to let her know that John's wife, Birthe, had taken her own life. How Hazel wished she could be there for her brother at this time of crisis. But she could pray for him, and she did. Crisis after crisis seemed to be rolling in like breakers on the seashore.

Hazel went to see how Iprim's leg was healing and knew at once that he was in pain. What had happened? One day Iprim, with his leg still in the splints, was climbing in the rafters of the house (as the children often did). One of the splints was making his leg sore as he moved around, Felis explained. Iprim fussed and cried and begged his dad to loosen the tie around the splints until Felis finally gave in. Before long the bones shifted. Poor Iprim was in pain and afraid to tell. By the time Hazel returned, his broken leg was nearly two inches shorter than the other one. Felis couldn't face another session of setting the bone, so Hazel suggested Felis carry Iprim to the hospital in Calapan. They prayed together, and Hazel left the decision to the family. Felis prayed. What should he do? He soon came to find Hazel. The Lord had indicated that they should set the bone again. He had come to ask Hazel to help.

"I went with a lot of quivering within. Felis had prepared 'Balite bark' and when we got to the house he made a bark splint—really like a cast. Dear Iprim just asked his Dad to pull gently and for me not to let go of his groin where I was holding. As it was nearly in position Iprim suggested we get the bark cast in place ready to apply, so we did and when the legs were the same lengths again we tightened the cast. He was so brave with tears running down his face from the pain. He said it wasn't painful any more and stretched out his hand to say, 'Thank the Lord.' I shook his hand and went home." A lot of prayer went up for Iprim and the splints stayed put!

By now, Hazel had spent twenty years painstakingly writing down Iraya and Tagalog words for the dictionary. Having seen the two pages that had been printed on computer, she knew it wouldn't be long before it was all printed. With mixed feelings, she placed it all in the hands of Mrs. Cabantog at the FEBC. This dictionary had been a large part of Hazel's life for so long. She knew she would continue finding new words for it. Would it ever really be done, or would there always be new words coming to light?

While she waited for the dictionary to be printed, Hazel and Pasita worked two to three hours a day translating the Book of Acts. Hazel immersed herself in Acts. She listened to the Exposition of Acts by David Pawson of England, and what she learned from him she passed on to the tribal folks in their morning Bible study. Hazel wanted them to have as much in-depth teaching on church history as they could and knew that they needed to have teaching from a variety of sources. Experience had taught her that she couldn't do it all herself.

Five of the pre-tuned radios (DZAS) were away being repaired. Hazel purchased an antenna to give better radio reception, and each morning she would play the programs loud enough so that the whole village could hear them through the walls of their bamboo and thatch homes. First came the news from 6:00 to 6:15 A.M., and then the Garden of Prayer for fifteen minutes. After that they gathered together for Bible study. Felis would often lead the whole group in a prayer meeting, but his method was quite different from what Hazel was used to. They would share prayer requests, and then everyone would pray aloud, in unison. Hazel had to cover her own ears to concentrate, but it did mean a shorter prayer meeting. The people were pleased when Hazel brought the repaired radios back so they could hear Christian programs again in their own homes.

Hazel was surprised when Neville Cooper found that the Cebuano language was almost as important as Tagalog in Mindanao. Could it be essential to church planting? Perhaps their new workers should begin learning Cebuano first rather than Tagalog. The workers decided on the course they wanted, and a request soon came for Hazel to set up the study course in Cebuano. She would just have to grade it and set the examinations for it. The request was stated as "a rather unexpected assignment," and being an assignment, Hazel didn't feel that she could refuse. The next day she instructed Felis and Pasita how to carry on translation, left paper and pen, and moved to the Language Centre to prepare.

She was disappointed to learn that the study books had not arrived yet. No one was even sure when they would come. A Cebuano speaker had not been lined up either. Hazel began looking at the schedule of studies and contents of the Tagalog course. Could it be used as a pattern? Four students were scheduled to arrive, but there was a lot of work to be done before the course would be set up. Finally Hazel went to Manila to borrow one set of textbooks from the Peace Corps in Manila. Their course had the Mindanao dialect in it, and Hazel was pleased with that. A schoolteacher on two weeks' leave helped Hazel put the lessons on cassettes, so Hazel was somewhat ready when the four new language students arrived.

Lindy and Nora, two of the language students were with Hazel one day, when a large flying ant landed on her plate. Hazel grabbed it, popped it into her mouth, pulled it out and stated that it was edible, and then ate it. Hazel continued to eat the ants and encouraged the girls to try them. The ants are fatty and have a distinctive flavour. Nora tried them but not Lindy. They had a good laugh and decided that, when other people were around and the ants flew in, they would all eat them. That should bring some shocked expressions! Hazel had a fun and easy way of introducing new missionaries to tribal life!

By examination time the dictionary was ready to be proofread. Hazel finished marking the Cebuano examinations and caught a ride to Manila. It took two days to check the entire dictionary. Hazel was pleased with the results. There were fewer than three hundred errors, not a lot considering the number of words recorded. Hazel delivered the corrections to the FEBC computer office and arranged to return in November to check the corrections.

During her break, Hazel visited the churches. She was relieved to find that everyone was well and happy in the Lord in Panalangdayan. It was a different story in Togaaw. The people there had stopped Sunday meetings. They were getting sick and were convinced it was a curse put on them by a "singer to the spirits." The Gisa group, too, was full of fear, being pulled between their old practices and living by faith. One Sunday a child had a *fit* and passed out. Spirit practices couldn't revive him, but when Felis prayed for him, he revived. The next Sunday, Felis himself had a seizure (which he had periodically). The people were frightened until he revived and continued his message.

The outcome was interesting. They wanted to know what had enabled Felis to get over the *fit* without the intervention of the spirits? They wanted to know about God's power to deliver from the "spirit singer," who, they believed, had cursed them. All their questions were answered from the Word. The Lord had used some unusual events to teach these people spiritual truths, and they began worshipping again. Within months, Hazel learned, as many as seventy met at Gisa. And they were not all believers. When Hazel returned to the language centre, Felis, Pasita and Mariano continued translating and finished two more chapters of the Book of Acts. Felis was also training five young men to prepare and deliver messages in other places. Two young people were teaching Sunday school under his guidance. It was exciting to watch the church begin to take shape and become independent, depending only on the Lord.

Interesting news from Canada encouraged Hazel. Her brother John was getting married again. He had peace in his heart regarding the past. Alberta had "parted with her gall bladder," and because of good nursing and God's grace, she "sprang back like a rubber band." She had painted the interior of the house, and a friend had given her a refrigerator and an electric stove. Hazel was relieved to know things back in Canada were fine.

Hazel was pleased to hear that Felis had decided to make a trip to Langkaan. The people there needed and wanted more Bible teaching.

"Why are you crying?" the other men asked Felis on the way up.

"I can hardly make it!" he replied, "And I was thinking about Auntie (Hazel) coming up here." Hazel's fall down the cliff on her trip to Langkaan the year before didn't seem to have had any lasting effects, but now, early in 1976, she began to have problems in one of the injured areas.

"The Dr. found a real sore spot in my groin and seemed to delight in pressing the lump and making it hurt," she stated in a letter home. She was advised to have it investigated in Manila, to drink more water and to reduce salt intake. As usual, Hazel's brain began working overtime. With thoughts of what might be happening, she left her things neatly sorted in Batangas in case she had to go home to Canada. Tests done in Manila were all negative. There was no lump! Hazel was relieved, but not so happy when the doctor told her to cut down on her workload.

By the middle of June thirteen missionaries were studying at the language centre, eleven Tagalog and two Cebuano. Hazel had seven different grammar lessons to teach and prepare each day and one period with Mrs. Cristobal, their Cebuano teacher. Cutting down on her workload was not that easy. Daphne Gibson took over assigning students to different churches in the area each Sunday, and as language examiner in Tagalog. It eased Hazel's mind to know that someone was still translating the Word in the Iraya dialect, but she did long to be helping.

Hazel eagerly scrutinised the pictures of John's wedding when she received them. Gladys, his new Danish wife, looked like a lovely person, and she had a fourteen-year-old daughter, Connie. Hazel was thrilled to hear that John had never been happier in his life. "When you come home on furlough next year I want you to know that you are especially welcome in our home," he wrote to Hazel. "Gladys is looking forward to meeting you." Hazel looked forward to that next furlough.

When the language students finished their course in August, Hazel was able to visit the Mangyan Bible School. This was where she had once been asked to teach. Felis brought her up to date on all the news. One couple had reconciled in answer to prayer and counsel. Another couple received comfort after their youngest child died. Rebeka was stronger and Pasita doing fine. Eight were ready to study baptismal classes at Togaaw. There was a new interest at Gelgey, meetings continued at Gisa, and Felis planned to go soon to openings in the interior. Hazel's heart was eased. Things were going on without her.

Tears coursed down Hazel's face when word came that Doris Elsaesser was not well enough to return to the Iraya work. This would leave the Iraya with no missionary who spoke the language. She wanted to return to the Iraya work, but more language students would be arriving in September. By November 26, nine were studying Tagalog, four Cebuano and three Bicol. Having Bicol added to the languages being taught meant extra work for Hazel, as well as learning the language herself.

Alberta was coming from Victoria to visit, and to travel home with Hazel when she left on furlough. They planned to take the long way home, visiting countries neither one of them had been to before. Alberta wrote to Hazel with the news that Mary Eleanor Allbutt had gone to be with the Lord after suffering with Alzheimer's for years. Hazel had known the Allbutts when they were missionaries in China. For many years, Ivan had been editor of China's Millions, a publication Hazel loved. His wife, Mary Eleanor, had suffered for a long time. Now she was at home with the Lord.

Within weeks, Hazel received another shocking letter. Alberta was engaged to be married—to Ivan Allbutt! That news caught Hazel completely off guard. Alberta assured her that she would still come for a visit. Hazel's hopes, to retire with Alberta in the wee house they jointly owned, were blown away. Alberta flew out to the Philippines the middle of December, and the longtime friends had a great time. But the time Hazel expected would be spent showing Alberta what wonderful things the Lord was doing, instead was spent shopping for hand-embroidered material for their dresses for the wedding. Hazel was to be Alberta's maid of honour. It was a bit of a surprise to Hazel when Alberta had all of her upper teeth pulled out in Manila. Hazel realised that it was a huge financial saving compared to having it done in Canada, but it did put a bit of a damper on their Christmas dinner. Hazel had to purée all of Alberta's food.

Now it was time for Hazel to wind things up again in preparation for furlough. She supervised the Cebuano examinations in Valencia, introduced the Manobo language study to the students there, handed over the Linguistic Examiner's job to Morven, celebrated an early sixtieth birthday with friends, and went to see Florence, who was now eleven years old. Hazel was thinking of her return before she even left the Philippines. She had a long talk with the tribal superintendent, Andreas Fahrni, about the possibility of working with the Iraya again, at least some of the next term.

Hazel and Alberta flew directly to Canada rather than leisurely visiting new places. True to his word, both John and Gladys welcomed Hazel to their lovely home, and even invited six of Hazel's friends to celebrate her sixtieth birthday there, February 11, 1977. Hazel's sister, Vi, was coming for Alberta's wedding on March 11, as well as Frances Williamson and several other friends. Hazel could hardly wait. She had beds for four and floor space for all the rest. (Hazel was always more comfortable on the floor anyway.)

On the day of the wedding, Hazel walked down the aisle in a pink embroidered, floor-length dress. Imitation rose buds in her hair matched her corsage of deep pink rose buds.

The bride was dressed in a long, sky blue, embroidered dress with a blue shoulder length veil. An arrangement of red roses covered the Bible she carried. After the ceremony, the bride and groom made a quick visit to Ivan's 102-year-old mother.

With Alberta married and her company gone home, Hazel was alone in her house for the very first time, and for the first time in twenty years she would be going on her deputation trip alone, with neither of her parents. She was thankful that the Lord provided friends to live in her house while she was travelling and a young couple to rent her house when she returned to the Philippines. She was back in Victoria for the Golden Jubilee of Central Baptist Church, the congregation that had so faithfully supported her on the field.

John and Gladys came to Hazel's for Christmas. They decorated a tree outside, then decorated other parts of the house and phoned both Irvine and Vi. "We had Danish Christmas supper the 24th and then Canadian Christmas dinner at noon the 25th after church at Central. We sit and chat a lot too," she wrote in a letter. Many things had changed in Hazel's life, but her relationship with her brother and his new wife was a good change.

Hazel had not given up on her plans for a world tour. Her yen to see new places had not quite been satisfied, so she took the long way back to the Philippines. Her first stop was in England, where she visited Doris Embery, Jean Pearce, and Dr. and Mrs. Broomhall. She also shared news of the tribal work at the year-end day of prayer at the home for retired missionaries. Margrit Furrer gave Hazel a full two weeks of pleasure in Switzerland, and her flight back to the Philippines took her to Athens, Dubai and Delhi. She even had time to look through the gift shops in Bangkok when they stopped there.

Now she was ready to throw herself back into the work, hopefully with her beloved Iraya people. But her dream was put on hold again. Her new assignment was with the Bicol language group, at Daraga, eighteen hours away.

# CHAPTER 20

## TO THE BICOL

Before Hazel went to work in the Bicol area, she wanted to see her spiritual children. She visited Anghel and Rosario at Kaagutayan and went up to the field, over seven river crossings, to find Rosing and her son. She spoke at the service in Kaagutayan on Sunday and then went back to Calapan. Hermann Elsaesser took her to Kasagi on his motor bike, and she had a wonderful visit with the people that night and at prayer meeting the next morning. Carlos' widow, Pakane, and her son were there.

She visited the other missionary women in the area and Alehandro guided her to Kaagutayan on a trail she had travelled only once before. What excitement! Felis talked quite a while with her, and she and Pasita talked until midnight. Hazel was pleased with Pasita's sweet character. "She is a wonderful Christian and so radiant and victorious even though Rebeka is still not able to sit or walk." Twenty-one baptised believers were there and weren't in a hurry to go home after the meetings. Felis and Pasita both committed again to helping her with translation work, and Felis was even willing to build an addition onto her house. Hazel hoped to be done with the Bicol work by July.

The Bicol area was southeast of Manila, not on the island of Mindoro. Daphne Parker, who had been the first missionary there, a year earlier, had to leave when her mother became ill, and Chris Harris, her co-worker, returned to England for medical help. Hazel moved into their residence. Ken and Norma Pullen, the newest arrivals, and Mike and Betty Harrison were all still learning the Bicol language. Hazel was there at their request to help prepare language courses, so that they could learn faster. Even while they studied the Bicol language, these couples were doing visitation, teaching Bible classes, and broadcasting over the Far East Broadcasting station. But it was all in Tagalog.

Hazel learned Bicol from the textbooks available, and, as soon as she caught up to the Pullens, she began work on grammar notes with more illustrations and clear explanations. Once she had sections four and five of the course done so the Pullens could continue, she concentrated on updating the first three sections. Lessons one and two would be the greatest challenge and more new workers were due in January. Hazel listened to Bicol news reports on the radio, and programs on farming and cooking, so that both the customs and the culture would be included in the lessons. Letty, a Christian girl, helped her by dictating conversations and expressions commonly used in the homes. Hazel was now reading through the Bible in the Bicol language. She set a goal of six hours a day in study. She was so busy and involved that February twenty-fourth almost passed unnoticed. It was the twenty-fifth anniversary of her arrival in the Philippines. She had worked in six different languages.

God, in His unique way, set up a meeting that would help Hazel immensely. Elsie and Rose stopped in. Rose needed to type up fifty proverbs and fifty riddles in Tagalog. That was no problem, but neither of the girls could manage Hazel's typewriter. Hazel ended up doing the job herself. Amazingly, as she worked, Hazel realised this was exactly what she had learned at Translators' Institute: using proverbs and riddles in translations. Hazel made carbon copies for her own use, and, in exchange for her assistance the girls promised to help her get some proverbs and riddles to use in the Bicol language course.

Hazel was finding it hard to sleep. Mt. Mayon, a volcano, was erupting. "Each night when it is clear you can see the lava flowing from the cone down the side of the

177

mountain. Each day all you see is the smoke. The path of the flow widens and new paths are formed. Whenever I wake during the night I look out at it. It never sleeps. One marvels at how long it can keep up the flow of lava." It was difficult to ignore such evidence of God's power, so visible at night.

Harrisons and Pullens were teaching ten Bible studies now and were almost overwhelmed when someone donated two hundred Bicol New Testaments. Letty was helping again, translating Tagalog language lessons into Bicol. Hazel wrote grammar notes for each lesson and made vocabulary lists for the Bible verses, health terms, proverbs and other items used. Drills for each lesson were translated, and, as usual, all these had to be checked with at least one other good Bicol speaker before they could be typed up. Hazel made ten carbon copies as she typed them, so that there would be enough copies for the students who arrived next. Finally, cassettes were recorded for use with the lessons.

Hazel grabbed at the chance to visit Buhi and learn more about the Negritos. She was amazed to meet Elmer Wolfendon in that isolated place. He had been at SIL in North Dakota in 1952, and was appointed to the Philippines a year after Hazel. He and Tom Mickle were surveying the Negrito area. Hazel accompanied them into a totally new territory and listened and watched with interest as they conducted their survey. She witnessed another exciting milestone when the first Filipino missionaries arrived. Working under the Association of Bible Churches in the Philippines, Sonia Mirabuenos and Cleta Castillo were on loan to the OMF to help establish a church in Daraga.

Hazel wasn't back in Mindoro by July, as she had planned. What she thought would be a few months working on the Bicol language was fast approaching a year. She took a holiday with the Sanglaps, and returned with renewed enthusiasm and a goal to be finished and leave Daraga by February 8, the end of a whole year here. It would not be easy to move back into tribal life after a year in Bicol, and what Hazel referred to as *soft* conditions.

Hazel began hearing rumours about the SIL wanting to do a survey of the Iraya group. The OMF had not officially admitted that there were enough Iraya-speaking people to make translation a priority, even though Hazel and others had done fairly in-depth surveys. There were great numbers of Iraya people further up the mountains, but there were great needs everywhere.

On top of this was the question of how much longer the Mission would allow Hazel to stay on the field. In one of her letters home Hazel writes, "If I am to retire after this term then before I leave the field it would be nice to have someone lined up to continue the job of Iraya translation." An understatement, of course! Hazel had a burning desire to see this translation work continue. Her heart wept for the Iraya tribal Christians, who struggled spiritually because they couldn't understand the Word.

Hazel finished recording the Bicol lessons, typed up grammar notes, and made necessary corrections. What she did not finish was reading through the Bicol Bible. Before she left the Bicol area, she made another trip to the Negritos area with Doming and Jeremias, Mangyan men who were opening a mission to the Negritos. The Lord was finally supplying the labourers everyone had prayed for through the years. In addition, five men arrived to start studying Theological Education by Extension, classes on personal evangelism. What they learned, they put into practice and gave reports each week as to what God had done through them. It was also an excellent way of training and putting more workers into the harvest field!

The morning of February 20, the workers in the area had prayer together with the Pullens in their new work in Tabaco. That afternoon Hazel assembled the Bicol Grammar Notes, added them to the file, and handed everything over to Betty Harrison, in charge of the Bicol language study. On

February 23, 1979, Hazel left by bus for Manila, a year and fifteen days after she had arrived. Her prayer request was to "pray as I adjust to tribal work again, recalling the language and getting back to a different kind of life after three and a half years away from it."

The issue of another Iraya survey was finally settled. SIL was not interested in a survey unless OMF was, and OMF was not interested. Hazel was glad! She did not want to spend more time on a survey that had already been done. She was planning a trip of another kind, though. When Hazel visited Margrit in Switzerland, they made plans for Margrit to visit Hazel before her next furlough. They would travel together to Switzerland, perhaps via the Holy Land. Perhaps Margrit would return to work with Hazel in the Philippines.

Hazel was amazed and amused when Margrit wrote that she was getting married—to a widower. Hazel's witty response to this was, "It sounds like anyone who has such plans (to vacation with me) had better be prepared to find a husband coming along to claim her and have plans changed. It HAS happened before. Really, I'm very happy about it and am sure God leads His own children aright."

Hazel wasn't surprised to get blisters on her feet after arriving back to the tribal work. Spiritually, things were in a slump. There was no outreach going on, except for occasional visits to family members in other areas. Rebeka was still not able to sit up alone, but was bright and well. No outsiders were attending Sunday services, so they were studying the Bible, book by book, with Felis teaching. Gillian had been giving studies in I Kings whenever she visited. Pasita told Hazel how much it meant to them to study new parts of God's Word. Hazel was encouraged when the men added a lovely translation room onto her house in Panalangdayan.

Hazel, Felis and Pasita began working on the Iraya translation of Acts where they had left off. They reviewed the translations Felis and Pasita had done on their own, and compared them to what Anghel had done in Kaagutayan over the years. They would work together for three hours most mornings, and then Hazel would spend most of the rest of the day recopying the translated work.

In May Hazel made a trip to Kasagi and was warmly welcomed. She walked to Alakaak to visit Elias and Lucing. Florence asked Hazel to write to her and wanted a New Testament. Hazel sent one to each of the three children. She visited Inchang, now at home in Kalamintao, still in a wheelchair. Then Hazel sorted her belongings in Calapan, picked up her belongings from Kasagi, and prepared to settle down in Panalangdayan.

Everyone was pleased to have her back, and, as usual, showered her with gifts of food. One gift was a mushroom called *the ear of a water buffalo,* but it was bigger than a water buffalo's ear. It had brown streaked worms in it, and according to Pasita, the worm was to be cooked and eaten with the mushroom! "They are there on purpose to make them taste especially delicious," Pasita added. Sure enough, it was delicious.

There was excitement in the village. For years these people had lived under the threat of having their children taken away to residential schools. Now, finally, Hazel obtained permission from the Superintendent of Schools to start a school, The Mangyan District Christian Elementary School in Panalangdayan, under Ann Flory's supervision. Forty pupils were on the list, so two buildings and two teachers were needed. Felis and his daughter, Milya, were trained to teach. Everyone breathed a sigh of relief. Their children were safe at last.

Florence, the premature baby Hazel had taken to her heart, was now a teenager! It caught Hazel off guard when Florence wrote her a sad tale of rejection and running away to live at a schoolmate's home. What was Hazel supposed to do? Andreas thought Hazel should go to Mamburao to see what was happening. Never in her wildest dreams had Hazel imagined this scenario, but the outcome was that Florence came to live with her. The whole village of Panalangdayan came to her aid. They decided that Florence needed to be with a family, and Florence could choose which family she wanted to live with. She chose Felis' family. After several weeks of homesickness, she settled in. However, there was a problem. Iprim, Felis' son, was close to the same age. The problem was solved when it was decided that Felis would still be reckoned as her father, but that Florence would live with Pasita. One positive aspect was that Florence had completed grade five, had been out of school for three years, and was able to teach when Felis needed her help in the school. Hazel hoped the problem was solved. She was more than ready for a holiday! It was quite a holiday. Hazel and Jeanie Dougan vacationed in Taiwan.

"Yesterday I returned from the most exciting trip I have had for years! The surroundings made me almost feel I was back in China," Hazel wrote. "We went to Taipei for the monthly prayer gathering of OMF workers of the area ... and south to Tainan where Frank and Ruth Lin entertained us well. Ruth and I went to China together and haven't met since 1947."

When she got back, one of the first places she visited was Bayanan, where she had been the first resident missionary in 1954. Some people were going on with the Lord, but many had fallen away. About ten minutes from the Mangyan Bible School was the water wheel that Andreas Fahrni had invented and installed at the waterfall. It generated electricity for lights for evening study and even for the dryer for their newly harvested rice. It was a wonderful blessing to the area.

The first draft of the Book of Acts was finished in December 1979. Hazel feared Felis would not be able to carry on much longer, but he was almost indispensable to the work. TB had damaged his bronchial tubes, and he had fluid in his lungs. Without him, the Iraya translation work would slow down considerably. Then the doctor suggested Hazel supplement his diet, with a vitamin pill and a glass of milk, every day when he came to work. That made a great difference. Translation began moving ahead quickly now. With Acts done, they moved on to Galatians, finished that in March 1980, and then reviewed Philippians and Mark.

While things were going well with translation, things were not going so well where Florence was concerned. A young man came along, wanting to marry her. Having Florence married would take a load off Hazel's mind, but Felis claimed he had the right to step in. He put a stop to the marriage, because Florence still had issues to work out with Iprim. Felis would allow Florence and Iprim to be engaged, perhaps in a year. Meanwhile, Felis would not allow Florence to go anywhere alone.

By September they were translating the Book of Romans. Pasita arrived early the morning they were to work on Romans 1:18-27, a portion of Scripture that is not easy to translate in any language. She started out rather hesitantly, almost as if she wanted Hazel to suggest the translation. It was not a new issue. This type of immorality was going on even among the Iraya. Gradually, with encouragement, Pasita opened up, and her translation was true and clear.

Permission was finally granted for Iprim and Florence to marry in October, and then they ran off and got married. They wanted to build a house and be the schoolteachers.

Hazel longed to see the entire Iraya New Testament translated. Book after book was being finished, but it wouldn't be done before her furlough. She began to talk about staying longer than her regular term. She would be sixty-four years old at furlough time. Delaying her furlough would depend on the mission doctor, and Dr. Hogben didn't think it was a good idea. She would, however, approve of Hazel's coming back after her furlough, if she were well.

If only there was someone else who had the same burning desire she had to see the Scriptures translated into the Iraya language. Then the Lord answered a prayer that had been on Hazel's heart for several years. Arlette Dombre, a French girl, had just finished her second Tagalog language course. She also had a passion for Iraya translation. Theo Herren, the Area Director; Andreas Fahrni, the Mindoro Superintendent; and David Fuller, Theo's Deputy – all sensed God's leading in this. Arlette had a good background of linguistic training, and could finish her Tagalog studies while Hazel was on furlough. Then they could begin working together. Praise the Lord! The two formed an instant bond.

Meanwhile, Pasita and Cesar worked faithfully with Hazel, and by July 18, 1981, the Gospel of Mark, Acts, Romans, Galatians and Philippians had been translated and recorded. Rejoicing, they sang the doxology and thanked God for His goodness in getting the recording done. Romans was even mimeographed and assembled. The afternoon of July 20, Hazel began to mimeograph the other four books with Morven's help. When they had finished mimeographing, stapling and putting the covers on, they had only to dry the stencils of Mark, spray them against mould and put them away. One hundred copies would be available for use in various areas during the year.

This time when Hazel flew from Manila, she went to Australia, where a group of missionaries and friends met her. She visited Melbourne, Sydney and Brisbane, Australia, and finally Christchurch, New Zealand, where she visited Morven's family. After almost a month Down Under, she flew home to Canada. John and Gladys, Ivan and Alberta, and Jeanie Dougan were waiting for her. John and Gladys were happy to have her with them. Gladys sewed beautiful dresses, blouses, nightgown, dressing gown and a lovely, long-sleeved suit for her. John insisted on buying her shoes to match. In Victoria, because her house was still rented, Hazel stayed with her niece, Doreen Wensley, and Frances Williamson came to visit.

Once the OMF Fall Prayer Conferences were underway, Hazel spent eight weeks travelling in the United States, visiting friends and supporters and enjoying Christmas with the Don Richardsons. "I slept in 21 different beds," she reported, "and the longest I stayed in one home was five nights." It was a hectic schedule, and Hazel loved every minute of it.

Technology was making huge changes in how things were done, and not only in Manila. When it was time to send out prayer letters, Central Baptist Church in Victoria (Hazel's home church) printed one hundred letters for her. In two days they were in the mail. What a change from her early missionary days! One of the most precious changes took place when she spoke at a prayer meeting at White Rock Baptist Church. Her brother, John, was with her and used his own projector to show her slides. It was his first prayer meeting, and he enjoyed it. Hazel was thrilled!

John and Gladys had celebrated Hazel's sixtieth birthday with her in 1977, and now she was in Canada for her sixty-fifth. John managed to find out who her closest friends were and invited them to a party. He also insisted that she make a suggested gift list. John met everyone who came by ferry or bus. Her gifts included things like adhesive bandages, elastic, and a folding water container. Hazel was well, and she would be going back to the Philippines! All her belongings were there, and so was her heart!

Conferences and missionary meetings, the Sixtieth Anniversary of Prairie Bible Institute (Three Hills, Alberta) and Vi and Bill's fiftieth wedding anniversary filled her summer. When it was time to leave, John repaired an $8.00 typewriter Hazel had purchased, bought her a small trunk, and drove her to the airport. She arrived in Manila on July 16, 1983. How long would they allow her to stay?

"At last, after so many years I am going to have a permanent partner," was the thought going through Hazel's mind. "I hope I can treat her right so she will stay." Hazel knew and had been told that she was too domineering. She had been told off for collecting so much junk! Co-workers were intimidated by the fact that she could get up so early, hike so far, eat so little, and still praise the Lord. Anyway, Hazel was determined that this partnership would work. After all, Arlette was the answer to all her prayers.

# CHAPTER 21

## RETIREMENT?

"What are the needs on the field?" a woman had asked Arlette. When Arlette mentioned the need to add another room on their jungle home, the woman offered to pay the entire cost ($200). Now they could each have a bedroom. Hazel was so glad to be back. Their headquarters now would be at San Teodoro, the place where Hazel had begun her work in the Philippines with Frances.

In contrast to their first house, the one rented for Hazel and Arlette now had wood walls, a proper stairway with a railing, and a corrugated-iron roof. It was all freshly painted. There were two bedrooms upstairs and one down, as well as a living room, a dining room, and a kitchen. The toilet facilities were just outside. A pump in the yard supplied good water, and they had electricity and a new refrigerator. There was even glass in the windows!

Hazel and Arlette made the ascent to Panalangdayan in the hottest hours of the day. Earlier letters had informed them that all the houses but Hazel's had been flattened by a bad typhoon. Food crops had been destroyed, and the Mangyan Development Program was helping. Relief funds were being channelled through the program, administered by the tribal people. They were curious to see if any of Hazel's belongings were left. Very little! Only the nylon mosquito net and a few other things seemed usable. All the cotton things were rotten. One tin of bedding was soaking wet, but, thankfully, she had bedding stored in another place. Her typewriter and kitchen knives had been stolen. Hazel was pleased to discover, though, that with some mending, the patchwork quilt that she had made in 1975 could be salvaged.

More than fifty adults and children gathered in the church to praise God for His faithfulness during the past year. Felis told how God had undertaken for them after the typhoons had destroyed crops and homes. Pasita explained how God had helped her meet the medical needs of the group. Arlette and Hazel shared how God had led them.

One of their first jobs would be to add another room on their house, but it didn't take long to find that living together in their wobbly house would be difficult. When Hazel got up during the night (and she did every night), her steps shook the whole place, waking Arlette. Adding a room would not be a good idea.

"Why not build a second house a distance away?" Arlette suggested. They both could do translation work without disturbing each other. Better yet, they would each have their own sleeping quarters. Meals, prayer, and fellowship could still be shared. So the supplies were ordered. Iprim was one of the ten carriers who brought in all the supplies for the new house. Florence's baby girl, Dina, was six months old, and as sweet as could be.

By September they were well into translating I and II Thessalonians. Hazel was shocked to learn that, in the excitement of getting the five books ready and copied before she left for furlough, Felis had been overlooked. All the copies were sold to others. Felis hadn't even realised they were available. He was not angry or bitter, but Hazel felt awful. She made sure that he had his own copy now, and he was very pleased. Felis had finally accepted his weak and sickly body, and realised that it was because he was sick he had time to help with the translation of the New Testament.

Suddenly, Hazel was called upon again to use her midwifery skills. Felis' daughter, Milya, was having a difficult delivery. Hazel relied on the Lord for help and turned the baby. The cord was around the baby's neck twice, but God enabled her to deal with this, too, and the baby rallied. Milya had a lovely baby girl. Every difficult birth was such a picture to Hazel of how the "babes in Christ" here struggled to survive spiritually. Many were growing and maturing, and it was exciting to see the local people taking up the ministry.

Alehandro had a suggestion for Hazel and Arlette. Could they start a study during the week to give them help preparing messages for preaching and personal work? They could! Twenty adults came to their first class on Saturday morning. They would use I Thessalonians, since that was the book they were translating. First, Pasita read a portion aloud. Everyone answered questions and then applied the Scripture to their own lives. This was a great help to the translation, too, and by the end of October 1983, they had finished I and II Thessalonians.

The next book to be worked on was I John. This brought up a translation problem. In the Iraya language, the only words for love imply bodily attraction. Clean is a condition they don't often experience physically, so the word is borrowed. Hazel was determined that this Iraya translation be absolutely clear so it could not be misunderstood.

Years earlier, working in the Hanunoo language, Hazel had preached on the text, "Owe no man anything, but to love one another." The following day a man appeared at her door saying he had come to pay his debt. Hazel was able to call for help, and the man ran away. Questioning one of the women later, she realised the wording she had used in her sermon was not perfectly clear and had obviously been misconstrued. The final wording they decided on now was, "Show God's love to one another." It was a good choice!

Ten people had come from a distance, wanting to be baptised. Felis taught them every afternoon all week. On Sunday it rained. They couldn't stay any longer, so Felis baptised them in the rain. Hazel watched with interest. Felis held the person's wrists against their chest with his right hand. With his left hand he grabbed a handful of hair, and made sure each one went right under the water. A praise service and the Lord's Supper followed. Ripe banana represented the bread and water symbolised the wine, served in cups formed out of leaves.

Amyano was helping Arlette get stories of life and beliefs recorded on her cassette recorder so that she could analyse the different affixes (additions to words) used in the stories. One word they had trouble with was "baptism." They finally decided on "tipped over in the water and raised up again." It was a long expression, but no one word in Iraya expressed what takes place when one is baptised. That and other terms had not yet been approved by the Bible Society, but it made sense to the Iraya believers who checked the translation with Hazel. On November 16, they finished the translation of III John and started Ephesians.

Arlette had a fever. Even after taking malaria medication, it didn't leave. Then she developed a sore throat, a cold in her head and chest, followed by dysentery and then hives. The doctor insisted that she stay in Manila until her fever went down. Hazel prayed fervently that Arlette would recover. They were making such good progress on finishing the New Testament, and she did not want to lose another co-worker. Arlette missed the lovely ham John sent for the girls for Christmas. Hazel was so relieved when Arlette came back.

Hazel wrote, "Translation work is progressing more slowly now. Pasita and I are working in the afternoons, checking the books already translated. Felis and I are revising Romans, while Galatians and Philippians will follow. Having Arlette to type all the manuscripts and back translations means I will be able to prepare much more than I could on my own. Arlette and I are designated to translation work and are not to be involved in other activities." After all those years, the mission had at last designated them specifically for Iraya translation! It seemed like things were slowing down, but the end was in sight.

Someone still needed to teach about church life and growth in the churches. In February 1983, Hazel and Arlette decided to take a week to visit villages on the other side of the island. There were very few people at home at the first place where they stopped, but those who were there wanted a Bible study in Iraya. It was an excellent way to try out their translations. They went on to Kasagi and stayed for Sunday, then on to Alakaak and Kalamintao, where Inchang cooked an eel for them. They had an Iraya Bible study there and then went on to Pambuhan. They were fairly close to where Huaning lived, so they visited him, too. Being blind, he relied much on the Christian radio programs, but his radio was broken. The missionaries took his radio and promised to get it repaired. Their next stop was at Kaagutayan, where they checked the translations with Anghel. Their aim was to have six books finished and ready for the Bible Society to check the first week in May. With great perseverance, they were able to finish all six books in time.

A portion of *100 Questions Answered From the Bible* had been translated into Iraya, but no copies had ever been made. It was such a great teaching tool. How much greater it would be in the hands of the tribal men burdened to go to Mayaas. What was stopping them from putting this literature into their hands now? Arlette typed the fifty-four questions already translated, while Pasita helped Hazel finish the rest, plus the Beatitudes, the Ten Commandments, and the Lord's Prayer. There was great rejoicing the day Cesar and Minis (Felis' son and his brother) were commissioned for the work, with Iraya literature in their bags.

Hazel took Felis and Pasita to Calapan with her to meet with the Bible Society representative from Manila. Checking went more quickly than expected, because their translation of the six books was almost perfect. Dr. Osborn preferred as little punctuation as possible—let the wording indicate sentence endings—but the words *this* and *that* had to be carefully selected. They had part of the checking process done. Hazel had already written out the English back translation (reading it in Iraya and writing it in English). Now, with Dr. Osborn following that transcript, he had her back translate the entire manuscript verbatim. If he had a question, they would stop so that he could discuss it with Felis and Pasita. They were very responsive and did well.

At the end of June Felis sent thirteen baptismal candidates to Arlette and Hazel to be questioned. They were absolutely clear about salvation. They scheduled the baptism for the next Sunday at Kadayangdangan. The trek took three hours over ridges and across streams, until they finally reached the river, where everything had been prepared. Two walls and an outside bench had obviously just been added to their church. Amyano gave a message, and then Felis spoke for a good hour. How wonderful they no longer had to wait for a man to come from somewhere else to lead communion. The tribal church leaders were now qualified to do it.

October 5, 1983, was a day that would be circled on the calendar. That was the day the computer took over mountains of time-consuming work! Arlette learned how to use it, and in a few hours she had the six translated books on the disk and copies printed. What had previously taken months of typing, and long trips to Manila, was now at their fingertips. Arlette helped demonstrate its use at Field Conference. Praise swelled from the missionaries, and prayer was fervent as this new equipment was dedicated to getting God's Word printed in tribal languages.

Perhaps there was a possibility that Hazel would see the Iraya New Testament finished before retiring. Her dedication in producing the Iraya/Tagalog/English dictionary had laid a foundation for the quick translations that now followed. Few recognised the years that she had spent recording every new word, painstakingly checking and rechecking cross references; writing and rewriting words by hand; and filing and upgrading the entire language.

Almost like a parallel to the birth of the Iraya New Testament, there were physical births. Florence gave birth to a baby girl on November 2, 1983. Hazel dressed her in a little shirt supplied by a missionary group in Moncton, New Brunswick. Only days earlier Hazel had helped to deliver twin boys. The first was a normal birth but the second baby was breech, and didn't breathe immediately. Time seemed to stand still as Hazel worked hard to clear his air passages. What a relief when he finally gasped that first breath.

Sometimes Hazel squeezed in time to care for herself. "I have just finished knitting kneecap socks. They are a pale green and are not only to keep me warm in this cold humid weather but also to keep the mosquitoes and gnats from biting." Arlette threatened to take a picture of her with socks up to her knees, topped with these green kneecap socks. Hazel refused. "Beauty is not my desire," she stated, "just comfort."

Christmas services over the years were almost a spiritual barometer of church growth in the village churches. This year, 1984, there were stories and special music in both Tagalog and Iraya. The offering was almost fifteen times the usual. Florence borrowed a guitar and sang for both the Christmas and New Year's services. It was almost impossible not to think back over the years to when the missionaries did all the preaching, and the music was atrocious! What a lot they had for which to praise the Lord.

Hazel hoped they could have I Corinthians, Galatians and Philippians ready to send to Dr. Osborn for review by the end of January. It was now 1985 and she was three years past her retirement date. Her medical checkup was scheduled for the end of January, and she could stay only if her health was satisfactory. Seven books of the New Testament had now been translated and checked by the Bible Society. Forty copies were printed. Hazel and Arlette got copies. The next copies went to Minis and Pasita, in appreciation for their part in getting the materials ready. Hundreds of people would want to buy the remaining number.

Hazel's excitement over the computer almost leapt off the pages of her prayer letter. "It is marvellous to see how the machine obeyed her (Arlette's) commands to put the right number of lines on the page with the right spacing, margins, page numbers and references. When all these commands were arranged on the disk, all Arlette had to do was to give the machine the right signal, attach the printing machine to the computer, insert the paper and it went to work." The downside of using the computer was that sometimes the electricity was off all day. Arlette spent a fair amount of time in Calapan, working whenever there was electricity. In spite of that, translation was moving ahead quickly.

There was still a need for Hazel to minister to the people. Thankfully, they now had the Lord to help them, but tragedy and problems were an unavoidable part of life. Iprim and Florence, like all tribal families, slept on the floor with their children. One night as he slept, Iprim rolled onto their wee baby, and she was smothered. Hazel mourned with them. It was a crisis that drew them all closer to the Lord, and the Word became a great strength to them.

Hazel was brought into another situation when Pasita and Talino wanted to get married. A huge problem revolved around an issue of culture. Pasita is a few minutes younger than Minis, her twin brother. If Talino and Pasita married, Pasita's spouse would be older than Minis' spouse, which was culturally unacceptable. Hazel could hardly believe this was happening. Even Minis, whom she considered to be firm in his faith, feared that a disaster would befall them if they violated the beliefs of their ancestors. But they were Christians now. Finally it was agreed that the Word of God must have the final say. Leviticus 18 lists forbidden marriages; this problem confronting them was not listed. In fact, many old Iraya customs were not listed there. Finally Pasita and Talino were allowed to marry. Their wedding was scheduled for Sunday after the service.

That week Pasita continued on with translation work. She taught Sunday school as usual and gave full attention to the worship service. There was no evidence of any preparation for the big event. The church service finished, it was time for the wedding feast. Pasita and Talino had purchased rice and all the ingredients for *pansit* (mainly noodles) but had made no arrangements for cooking it. Suddenly they needed more pots. They needed wood for the fire. The men were mobilised to get wood, and it was 4:00 P.M. by the time the food was cooked.

Hazel sat with Pasita's family under the shade of the trees and wondered why no one offered her food. She saw Felis set some pots of rice and noodles in the grass to one side and then take them to his house when the other food was gone. Then everyone went home. Alone at her house, washing the dishes she had loaned to them, Hazel was feeling a bit bewildered, even a bit hurt. Then Grandpa arrived with a huge dish of rice and a double serving of noodles. Suddenly it became clear. She was part of the bride's family.

Something else puzzled Hazel. The Manila Office asked if she was planning to go on furlough July 1985? Why were they asking again? She had told them the previous year that she planned to stay until 1986. Dr. Hogben hadn't found a reason why she shouldn't stay that extra year. Hazel secretly hoped she could extend it longer than that, until the Iraya New Testament was completed. Translation was going so well that perhaps it was possible. Could she even stay to see the whole Bible translated into Iraya?

At the end of March 1985, they had I Corinthians, Galatians, and Philippians ready for Dr. Noel Osborn of the Bible Society to check. Pasita was pregnant with twins, so this time Hazel took Amyano and Minis to Calapan with her. They worked from Monday to Friday, and finally all three books were ready for Arlette to correct on the computer.

Right in the midst of their push to finish the Iraya translation came a wonderful, encouraging celebration. The Hanunoo New Testament was finished and in print. Andreas Fahrni took a group, including Hazel and Amyano, down to Manaol for the dedication. In the heat of the day, they climbed to Tarubong to find Hanunoo people from every place in the entire area milling around. Pastor Guererro of the Bible Society, and Daphne McKenzie of OMF Publishers (who printed it), represented their missions. Missionaries Theo and Maria Herren, Andreas and Ruth Fahrni, Jim and Penny Wallace, Ann Flory, Hazel, and Martha Blair joined Elly and Frances Bezemer for this momentous occasion.

During the ceremony they were asked who helped with the translation. Hands went up all over the place. It took Hazel only seconds to realise that everywhere Elly ministered, she had gathered people to help her in the evenings. They had all shared in the translation work.

It was amazing, too, how the translation of the Word had influenced these Christians. The Hanunoo churches had already sent their first missionaries to the Negritos in the Bicol area. Jeremias gave a wonderful report of what God was doing there. After the dedication prayer, New Testaments were offered to the people even if they didn't have the thirty pesos to pay for them. Crowds of Hanunoo people received them with delight. The joy written on their faces was priceless! It was an incentive to push forward with the Iraya translation. Some day the Iraya people, too, would celebrate.

With Pasita's help they managed to finish translating II Corinthians, just before her babies arrived. Hazel was there to help, but the first baby was born on the ground at the outdoor toilet. Pasita carried her in. Two hours later when the placenta had not come, Hazel tied and cut the cord. The next day when the placenta had still not come, nor had the second baby, Hazel advised Amyano to have Pasita carried out to the hospital in Calapan. Arlette gave him money for expenses and an hour after their arrival at the hospital the second baby, a boy, was born. The first placenta was infected. Another day, the doctor stated, and they would have lost Pasita.

God's healing power was becoming real to these people. Felis was able to help translate I Peter most days. He was much better physically but was still using his cane. That was not good enough for Jeremias. One day he asked Hazel if it would be all right for him to pray for total healing for Felis! He prayed and the cane wasn't needed anymore. Felis' heart was full of praise for God's healing. The Word literally came alive to those who were helping with translation. They now claimed the authority to renounce the works of Satan and command him to depart in Jesus' name. Felis stated that, since the studies about these matters, he had had release from bondage in several areas and was teaching his family to deal with these matters as well.

Hazel began to downsize now in preparation for retirement. She gave her Bible school notes and Bible commentaries to the Philippine Missionary Institute and the Mindoro Bible Centre. She had saved every prayer letter she had written and many letters she had received. Now she felt she should dispose of most of them. As she burned old letters, she was deeply touched by the amount of time and money people had spent keeping in touch with her.

Minis, Amyano, Hazel and Arlette studying.

Minis took over from his brother, Felis, in helping with translating. He did well, even with the hard spots in II Peter. The Lord's hand seemed to be on that entire family. The Book of Jude followed, and the Committee asked that Revelation be next. Hebrews and James remained to be translated. Matthew, Luke and John wouldn't be so difficult, as much of it paralleled Mark, which had been completed first. Then all the New Testament would be mimeographed. By November Arlette had a laptop computer, which meant that they could enter the translations as they went along, right there in Panalangdayan.

Hazel had a strange feeling in her chest. She had experienced this same sensation a month earlier in October, but it lasted only about half an hour and went away. Dr. Medina said that it was angina, nothing too serious, and gave her medication. But Dr. Hogben sent Hazel to Manila for an ECG. It was February 1986, and Hazel was not prepared for the news Dr. Hogben gave her. Her health was precarious. She should arrange to leave Mindoro immediately!

"The way Dr. Hogben spoke," Hazel wrote home, "she thinks my departure for glory is imminent or at least the time when I will not be able to look after myself. Even getting my teeth repaired before going home was frowned on. The main thing is that I leave the Philippines alive!" Hazel was willing and ready to die on the mission field and said as much. That would not be a problem, the doctor replied. However, the likelihood was that she would be incapacitated, causing a great deal of difficulty for everyone else.

Hazel began to make plans to fly home late in April. At least she could go with a free heart. Arlette had learned the language and ways of the Iraya. She also had a passion for the people and translation.

All of her belongings were carried out to San Teodoro where she sorted and repacked. Andreas returned from the Area Council meetings with three items of news. First, Roswitha Vollemer, studying Tagalog in Batangas, was coming to work with Arlette. Second, he had requested that Hazel be allowed to stay till Field Conference the middle of May. Third, during that time she would stay with Caroline Stickley in Manila, instead of at the Mission Home.

Hazel handed all of her Iraya materials over to Tom Tweddell, whose parents had been a part of the Iraya ministry. She sold her typewriter and a camera. Hazel was so glad to have Arlette with her that last day in San Teodoro. In Calapan the area missionaries gathered for prayer and a farewell for Hazel. Each one wrote out a Bible verse and a memory concerning her.

"Dear Hazel, I give this verse to you. 'Sing, O barren woman, you who never bore a child; burst into song, shout for joy, you who were never in labour; because more are the children of the desolate woman than of her who has a husband, says the Lord.' Isaiah 54:1. What a comfort for you to know this is true for you. Thank you for your love, steadiness, diligence and prayerfulness, it's been a challenge to me, a young missionary just starting out. Love, Debbie Witherow"

"Dear Hazel, We will always remember you as long as our memories will last! Thank you for all you have done and been during your many years on Mindoro. You have fitted in so well and have never made life difficult for us. Lovingly, Andreas and Ruth"

"Dear Hazel, When I think of you, the pictures that come to mind have to do with the romance of missionary life. I see you pulling flannel underwear out of a trunk that had probably seen so much of what missionary biographies are made of. Or telling us how you got very happy on over-ripe jam or taking those old coins out of China in a kettle. But laced through it I see a simple personal faith in God. A faith that didn't tell us you didn't have enough food when we all came to visit - you told God and He quietly provided. Thank you, Love Gail. And thank you that you care for our family"

Hazel wrote her last OMF prayer letter in May 1986. She mentioned that she was introduced to the Iraya tribe the day after her arrival in Mindoro in 1953. Now, she concluded, less than a third of the New Testament was yet to be translated into Iraya. Hazel was now feeling what a young missionary expressed when he had to evacuate from China: "The trouble is, my heart has not yet got its exit visa." One hundred and thirty OMF missionaries working in the Philippines were at the Field Conference. The theme was "Refreshing Encounters with God, with Ourselves, and with One Another."

"This morning in the service of worship," Hazel wrote, "it struck me that this is my last Sunday in the Philippines. I was a bit tearful for a while. The OMF team had a farewell for Norman and Mavis Blake who retire in September, and also for me. I received a huge (trunk-size) wooden chest inlaid with mother-of-pearl."

She had more paper matter to take home than she planned. "But after all," she stated, "my work has been with papers and will continue to be as long as I'm able to cope." Her brother John, Ivan and Alberta, the Marvin Dunns, the Doug Shortts, the John Toops, and Anita Troop met her when she arrived in Canada. What a warm welcome! Men from Central Baptist Church were busy painting the exterior of her house when she got to Victoria. Mrs. Fleury had the kitchen nicely arranged with a good meal waiting. Cyril and Doris Weller and Eileen Singleton, all retired in Victoria, came to welcome and encourage her. With the help of a couple of men, her furniture was soon in place and boxes brought down from the attic. Gifts of money, food, and offers of help with yard work, were pouring in. Hazel had enough special gifts to purchase a used washer and dryer, and a $500 gift from the church was designated for renovations.

Her first priority, of course, was to see her doctor. He didn't seem too concerned about her health, but arranged for her to see a cardiologist. Hazel kept herself busy and her mind occupied until her appointment on August 5. She also kept the mail service busy between Canada and the Philippines as she continued to work on the Iraya translation. She checked Matthew and prepared suggested translations for phrases in Hebrews, which would be translated next. The Gospel of John would be done last.

Hazel kept her August appointment with the cardiologist and then had to wait again for the reports to be returned to her own doctor. She was stunned with the results.

# CHAPTER 22

## CHINA AGAIN

The cardiologist's report showed no problems with her heart. Dr. Cox stated that he would back her up if Hazel wanted to return to the Philippines. Hazel had a lot of thinking to do. "I am not planning to go unless the Lord definitely indicates that I should," she stated. Now that there was nothing wrong with her heart, she was able to get her dental work done. It came to over $2000, which she paid with money "saved over the years." She also began the daunting task of sorting through not only her own things, but her parents' things, as well. She found old Bibles stored away. One belonging to her father had an inscription: "A present from Grandma, Annie L. Page, January 1898." She and Vi decided to have it rebound. Another Bible had belonged to her sister Florence. Written inside was: "March 18, 1928, from Dad and Mother."

There was nothing to stop her from throwing herself back into the Lord's service. When the OMF Alumni Prayer Conference took place at Cultus Lake in September, Hazel was there. She even stepped in and led one of the seminars when the scheduled missionary couldn't be there. Then she enjoyed Expo '86 with a group from the Conference.

Hazel still fit into her maid of honour dress and wore it for Ivan and Alberta's tenth wedding anniversary celebration. Since their marriage, Alberta had turned the deed for the house back into Hazel's name alone. Then a group of

OMF folks helped Frances Williamson and her twin sister celebrate their eighty-third birthday.

Arlette's schedule was to rotate between France and the Philippines every few months. Hazel was thrilled when she arrived in Canada in August of 1987 to visit. There was not much silence in Hazel's home as the two caught up on news. They checked Hebrews and Revelation together and found it much easier than doing it via the mail service. After a furlough in France, Arlette was scheduled to study Hebrew in preparation for Old Testament translation and return to Mindoro in November 1988. The very sound of that was music to Hazel's ears. Old Testament translation! In December the translation of Luke was approved by the Bible Society, so just Matthew and Revelation still needed to be checked with believers in Panalangdayan.

Hazel spent Christmas with John and Gladys. Then, out of nowhere, came a phone call from Dr. Jim Taylor, General Director of OMF. Would Hazel be interested in going to China? An organisation called The Friends of China had openings for English teachers. Her heart, both physically and spiritually, was ready to go immediately, but Hazel prayed about the decision. She got in touch with The Friends of China. There were jobs available for her; it was only a question of time and place. What irony! Early in her life the Lord had burdened her heart for the Chinese people. Now she had the opportunity to return to China to teach English. Physically she was fine. There was no reason why she shouldn't go. So, yes, she'd be glad to go to China again. January 27, 1988, was her flight date.

Hazel couldn't help but chuckle over the difference between the outfit list of 1946 and this one in 1988. "Many of the things I took with me the first time I went to China were never used," Hazel stated, "the light-weight union suits, fingerless gloves (which she couldn't even find) or the bed pan and enema set." This time she took only what she needed and used everything she took. It would be different going to Communist China. She was reminded of rules laid down for her correspondence with friends when she left China so many years ago. Now she had to give those same guidelines to anyone who would be corresponding with her. "Most mail entering and leaving China is censored at both the point of entry, exit and at the local level. Avoid using envelopes or letterhead papers that indicate a church, mission or Christian organisation. Use non-religious vocabulary in your letter. Do not send prayer letters, missionary magazines, church newsletters or tapes. Do not ask questions about opportunities to witness, meet believers, give your literature or share Christ. Do not publish anything from your friend's letters."

Hazel could hardly believe that she was really back in Hong Kong. She felt so at home. Colin Johnston, a former OMF missionary in the Philippines, met her. It was much hotter than she remembered, so one of the first things she did was shed some layers of clothing. Hazel had a book to read in preparation for the new workers' retreat and orientation session. She read her book, then gave some of the other candidates an hour's help with Chinese, at their request. The classes on Chinese history brought her up-to-date since she had last been in China.

The No. 2 People's Hospital in Wenzhou was where she would be teaching English. Before her teaching job began, Hazel celebrated her birthday. It was great to be in China, but the Lord had prepared another birthday treat for her. Don and Miriam Stephenson and Lillie Jonat, friends from Victoria, were in Kowloon with a tour group. Hazel joined them there for a birthday meal.

Hazel opened a bank account at the local branch of the Bank of China and met with one of the hospital directors. Her room and board would be supplied. She was both surprised and disappointed when, a few days later, she was informed that her job was not available. The hospital was designated as a training institute, not a teaching centre, so the Education Bureau would not grant the hospital permission to have an English teacher. The hospital did pay her hotel bill and gave her a month's salary.

She was certain that the Lord had brought her back to China, but for what? Without a job, she could not change her visitor's visa to a worker's permit. One of the other places that had contacted her about teaching English was The Shanghai Institute of Science and Technology Management. And they still needed an English teacher. Three officials of the Institute came to the hotel to meet Hazel when she arrived in Shanghai, and she was soon welcomed as their fourth English teacher. Two Americans and one Canadian had registered the day before. For eight days she stayed with English-speaking Tim and Polly. It was the beginning of a lifelong friendship.

Hazel's two-bedroom apartment in the Institute had heater, air-conditioner, cleaning and laundry facilities. "It is better than I ever dreamed of," wrote this gracious woman, who had spent the past thirty-three years living in thatched huts. Hazel's previous experience in China made her feel right at home. She loved shopping in local markets, although it was frowned on, since there was a special canteen for the foreign teachers.

"The book I am to teach from is good. It is American, and I will also learn from it," she wrote. By March she was teaching four hours a day, four days a week. She taught Oral English to sixty students, all highly trained in science and technology. She felt a little inadequate for the job, but some of her students had studied English for up to ten years and had formed a few bad habits that needed to be replaced with good ones. One of the first things Hazel did was to record each student as they introduced themselves. Three evenings a week Hazel would have groups of six or seven come to her apartment for "Free Talk."

Within months of her arrival in China, Hazel was admitted to hospital in Shanghai with bronchial pneumonia. After a seven-day regimen of penicillin, she was released with instructions for a further week of sick leave. In spite of her absence, her students had made good progress and passed their exams. At the end of the eleven-week course, she recorded them as they introduced themselves again. The improvement was amazing and encouraging.

Hazel's nephew, Bill, and his wife, Trish, landed in China for a holiday, just in time for Hazel's vacation in July. Hazel was thrilled to spend two weeks in Beijing and Shanghai with them, touring The Forbidden City, Temple of Heaven, Summer Palace, Great Wall, Ming Tombs and Red Square. She had a wonderful holiday. When they left, she thought it would be fun to visit the places where she had ministered so many years ago. But times had changed. When she arrived in Kunming Province, she was disappointed to find that Wuting, Paoshan, and Longling were not open to foreign visitors.

Teacher's Day at the Institute was the time they recognised and honoured their teachers, and Hazel was seated at the head table. Several teachers were recognised for twenty-five or more years of service. Hazel was surprised to be praised for her contribution as an English teacher. She was presented with an ornate certificate, and a complete Chinese writing set. It would soon be time for her to return to Canada, but she already had two more job offers in China.

Another issue was pulling at her. Ivan had passed away and Hazel's good friend, Alberta, was quite sick. In the light of the wonderful care Alberta had given Hazel's father, should she go home and look after Alberta? By the time the letters flew back and forth, Alberta was feeling better. In December Hazel went to the Shanghai Boiler Works (SBW) to see about the job of teaching English there. They were even willing for her to spend a bit longer in Canada and begin teaching the first week in April. Hazel flew back to Canada by way of the Philippines.

"Our house in San Teodoro hummed with activity. No less than fifty people of all ages came from Panalangdayan to see me. Imagine the joy to see my Florence and Iprim and three wee girls." Their new baby girl was named Miriam. Felis had passed away, but Minis, Tasya and their eight children, and Amyano and Rosalina and family all came to visit. On Monday Pasita, Oding, Pasyo, and families came. "What a good time I had. They had come out on very muddy trails, part of the time in the rain, just to see me." Amyano looked up at Hazel as they visited and said, "Auntie, how is it you look younger and we all look older?"

Hazel, back in Canada in February, visited with John and Gladys and Vi and Bill, and then flew back to Shanghai at the end of March. This time she would teach in the Shanghai Boiler Works. She settled into a nice apartment in the same building as the International Office of the Boiler Works and quickly made friends with the staff. It was only a ten-minute walk to her classroom.

Hazel had been teaching two and a half months in Shanghai when students began protesting for freedom and democracy in China. On June 4, 1989, troops and tanks stormed Tienanmen Square in Beijing, and a massacre ensued. Shanghai students launched a surge of demonstrations in response, blocking all the roads to prevent the military from entering Shanghai. They did not want a repetition of what happened in Beijing. The Shanghai Boiler Works (SBW) sent a car to fetch Hazel on June 7. All "Friends Of China" associates were required to leave for Hong Kong immediately. The wind whipped through the broken back window of the car as they drove away. For the second time in her life, Hazel was being evacuated out of China.

A cable from Ottawa advised all Canadians to leave. A plane would arrive on Friday to take evacuees to Tokyo. Hazel still had her return ticket direct to Canada and that would be so much easier. She went to the airport, only to find that the flight she wanted had been cancelled. By the time she went home, finished packing, and returned to the airport, the planeload of Canadians was gone. She finally got another flight to Tokyo and then on to Vancouver. Less than a month later, everything had settled down, and Hazel was back in Shanghai to finish out the term.

This year on her holiday in September, Hazel and her Chinese friend, Daisy, went by ship up the Yangtze River. High rugged cliffs towered above them on both sides of this amazing river valley. How could people not recognise the spectacular creative powers of God in this part of the world? The Boiler Works made contacts in Wuhan to help them find a hotel room, food and a car. A highlight of the trip was a visit to an exhibition of scientific accomplishments of the past forty years (since the Communists took over China). They visited East Lake, one of China's largest lakes, and climbed 750 steps to visit temples on the top of a hill. Some of the places she saw were thousands of years old.

Hazel welcomed twenty new students for eleven weeks of study, up until Christmas. On Christmas Day, Tim and Polly took Hazel to the former CIM church, and the pastor and his wife took them to another church, where they minister to thousands. The Lord was at work in China.

The next class started in January 1990, and would also last eleven weeks. Hazel had noticed that students who walked with her to school and back each day made better progress than those who never walked with her. She decided to require all the students to take their turn walking with her, and also to come to her apartment for an hour, twice a week. When the course ended, the management was pleased with the excellent progress their workers had made in oral English. This year she watched the Chinese New Year's Eve fireworks from the seventh floor of the hospital, where she was being treated for stomach problems. She was soon well again.

Hazel flew back to Canada in time for the Fiftieth Wedding Anniversary of Irvine and Bessie. Her medical checkup was good, she had renters for her house, and a job was waiting for her again at the Shanghai Boiler Works. She was back in Shanghai in August. Everyone in the International Office was pleased to have her back. The temperature was 33° C, so she was especially thankful for the air conditioning in her apartment. Twenty new students began classes in September. Sixteen of her students had studied English for several months but had never had conversations with a foreigner. Hazel would soon rectify that! The Eleventh Asian Games were on in Beijing, so they became the topic of discussion during free talk. Hopefully, they would eventually be able to discuss various subjects of interest. She taught three hours each morning, Monday through Thursday, at the SBW, and two and a half hours in Shanghai on Saturday afternoon. Things were changing again in China and by law she could no longer stay overnight in Shanghai with Tim and Polly. She still felt safe. The Canadian Consulate General invited her to their Christmas dinner in Shanghai on December 8. It was her only Christmas dinner, since Christmas landed on a school day that year. It was school as usual.

One of her students asked if Hazel could teach them "Silent Night." Since they asked, of course she could. So they sang it often, as well as "Joy to the World." She gave them gifts of handkerchiefs and cash. The hanky means sadness and weeping, so the custom was to give money with it or you would break a friendship. In her spare time she had been busy making necklaces to give to the women of the office. Then on December 28, the Boiler Works treated all 6,000 workers to a bowl of noodles, a pork chop and fish.

Hazel was still checking the Iraya translations Arlette sent from the Philippines and answering questions about the choice of words. It was December 1990, and Florence was twenty-five years old. Rosario, Anghel's wife, had died. Because of the dates of the Chinese Spring Festival, Hazel would finish one class on February 7 and begin the next on March 1. It left just enough time to go to the Philippines.

Arlette was finishing I Corinthians on the computer, the last book to retype before the final check. Hazel read through Matthew and Mark, and they discussed parts of it. Arlette and Hazel and Spring (Arlette's new fellow worker from Hong Kong) travelled to San Teodoro and the next day

207

climbed to Panalangdayan. Hazel was 74 years old. She found that her house there had been partially destroyed in a typhoon, and it was being used to store school supplies. They were using the church as a school, too. Hazel visited all the homes and cuddled any child who was brave enough to come to her. She read through the Iraya New Testament and checked questions with Minis and Amyano. On the way back to town, they called at Kaagutayan to see Anghel and to pray with him. He looked much fatter than when Hazel had last seen him. Rebeka was too heavy now to be carried around, but was well looked after at home. Spring remarked that she had never seen Iraya people cry, but Florence, Pasita and Anghel all cried when they greeted Hazel. Sunday, at Panalangdayan, they asked Hazel to speak on the Great Commission.

"Going up to Panalangdayan my legs were strong and my breathing normal and I enjoyed the familiar sights," Hazel stated. "The sun was hot and the trail dry so no leeches were in sight. Going down on muddy trails, many leeches crawled up on my stockings but Spring was right behind me and alerted me so that only two drew blood." While she was in the Philippines, Minis, Amyano, Arlette and Hazel made the final corrections, and the translation of the Iraya New Testament was finished. They prayed fervently that many Iraya people would understand the Gospel.

The Mindoro Field Conference took place while Hazel was there, and she was thrilled to attend. Hazel would return to China for this next session, fly back to Canada in August, and, if all went well, come back to the Philippines in September for the dedication of this New Testament that had been on her heart for so many years.

Several of her new students in Shanghai had not studied the books assigned, but within three weeks they had all passed the oral test on the first half of Book I. Hazel was generous with her storytelling and taught her students about Canadian and Filipino culture. When the SBW planned a trip to Wuxi, Hazel, six Filipinos and two newspaper correspondents from Shanghai took the trip, and each brought home a five-pound bag of Wuxi's famous peaches.

It was becoming more difficult each year to live under the Communist regime. Every time Hazel visited her friends in Shanghai, she felt that she was putting them at risk. Sooner or later she would have to retire or, at least, give up full-time work. When she left China this time, it was hard to say good-bye. She probably would not be coming back.

Hazel teaches English to Chinese

# CHAPTER 23

## A DEDICATION

Hazel had turned seventy-four in February 1991. Now, in September, she was back in Mindoro, hiking up the jungle trail again, carrying a heavy load on her back. The weather was lovely, and the trail was good. Finally, for the last part of the trek, someone took her pack from her. Mindoro had been home to her for most of her life.

Her time was not consumed with translation today, and she had lots of time to visit. But that was not the reason why she had returned. The Iraya New Testament was in print, and the dedication was just days away. Her lifelong dream was finally fulfilled.

Most of the Mindoro missionaries, the group that had been Hazel's family on the mission field, gathered in Calapan on September 10, for a day of prayer. In one sense, it was a day of reunion, but it was also a day of celebration, as copies of the long-awaited Iraya New Testament were passed around. The dedication would take place September 20, in Talosian. Today the mission family had met to bathe that upcoming event in prayer.

Talosian was a lovely place for the dedication. An open shelter about 18' X 30', with banana leaves for the roof, had been prepared. Long tree trunks made up the six benches in the main part of the chapel. All along the sides were bamboo benches. It was a perfect spot. The surrounding hillside made a natural amphitheatre.

The day before the dedication, a happy, excited group—Florence, Iprim and their four children—accompanied Hazel and Spring down to Talosian to decorate. They hung a huge banner, prepared by an Irayan believer, across the front of the chapel. It portrayed an open Bible on the upper right end and a head of rice on the other, depicting both the physical and spiritual food of the Iraya people. Across the centre was printed PAGTATALAGA ng BAGONG TIPAN sa wikang IRAYA (Dedication of the New Testament in the Iraya Language), 09, 20, 1991.

Florence, Iprim and daughters

That night, as she had for most of her life, Hazel slept on bamboo boards. Even with a big mosquito net over her, Hazel didn't sleep much. It wasn't that the bed was hard. She was excited! The moon was bright. People bustled about the village all night, preparing food for the next day. The men killed and dressed a pig, and the women cut it up. At 3:00 A.M. they began to cook. As the rice was finished, they put it into bags, while the meat continued to cook.

It was hard for Hazel to believe that it had been thirty-five years since she first began to work with the Iraya people. What miraculous things the Lord had done in that time. Junior, the leader of the Tribal Church Association, arrived with printed programs, and name tags for the visitors. Others came struggling up the last wee climb, damp with perspiration and wet from washing shoes, socks and feet at the last stream crossed. Dear friends, old and young, were ecstatic to have Hazel back with them. Dr. Arichea from the Bible Society gave a moving message from the Word. Hans-Hermann Heldberg brought congratulations from OMF, along with his wife, Erika.

Iprim, her dear Iprim, recited a poem he had written for the dedication. Memories of setting his broken leg ran through Hazel's mind. Today he stood before the crowd, a mature Christian and a wonderful father. She was so proud of all her spiritual children. Young people from the local church sang the very appropriate song, "Wonderful Words of Life." The most significant part of the celebration, for Hazel, was when Minis read passages from the new Iraya Scriptures.

Dedication of the Iraya New Testament, September 20,

Fourteen New Testaments were presented to guests and translators. Minis and Amyano received copies. The brilliant smile on Hazel's face was one of pride, not in herself, but in these tribal people she loved so much, as she presented a New Testament to Pasita. The feast and the fellowship were pure joy to Hazel's heart. Sadly, others who had shared so much in the translation work were not there. Felis was at home with the Lord. Anghel was waiting for someone to come with a carabao sled to pick him up. They forgot. How he cried when he realised he had missed the dedication.

The following Saturday Hazel visited Anghel. An old man, he lived now in the new government housing project, thirty houses on cement floors. Then Hazel and Spring began visiting the churches. Sunday they went to church at Kaagutayan, where Hazel spoke in Iraya about God's Word. Monday morning they went on to Bayanan. Their arrival had been announced, by the radio station, now completely run by a Tagalog technician and tribal broadcasters. Everyone was waiting for them. At Ayan Bukug, a crowd came to greet Hazel, their first missionary. They gathered in the church to sing and read the Scriptures together once more. A trio sang. What a contrast to years long past, when each person sang their own melody at their own pace. They prayed together (in unison, of course) for the revival of spiritual life there and for their two outreaches. Ranak, who had so impressed Hazel with his quick learning as a young lad, closed in prayer.

This time, when Hazel left the Philippines, she knew her work there was done. Now it was up to others to take this Word she helped translate and spread it abroad. Leaving the Philippines this time was one of the hardest things she had ever done. But the love of the tribal people would forever be in her heart.

The beautiful carved chest, inlaid with mother-of-pearl, her retirement gift from the missionaries in the Philippines, sits in a corner of her little house in Victoria. Inside are treasures from the tribal areas. Her spare room, which houses her computer, is decorated with Filipino artifacts. Hazel has technically retired, but as was once said, not retired, redeployed!

One corner in her house is heaped with boxes of cotton yarn, rolled bandages and packing supplies for The

Leprosy Mission. Whenever she has a few minutes, Hazel is knitting bandages for The Leprosy Mission. Another corner and several drawers are full of stamps she is preparing to sell for missions. All the stamp dealers in Victoria know her, as she searches out the best prices.

Hazel was scheduled for minor surgery in Vancouver early in March 1992. Just days earlier, her dear friend, Alberta, had a stroke and was in hospital in Vancouver. Hazel planned to visit her the day after her own surgery. But God had other plans. Immediately after her surgery, Hazel felt compelled to go! And she did. Mere hours before Hazel's arrival, Alberta had suffered a massive heart attack. When Hazel talked to her, Alberta opened her eyes and her face lit up in a most beautiful smile. "I want to enter in," she said, then added, "I should have said, I want to go out." In a wavering voice, Hazel sang to her friend, "There's not a friend like the lowly Jesus, No, not one," as Alberta slipped away into the presence of the Lord.

Just weeks later, on March 26, Hazel's brother John was called Home, too. Hazel was thankful that she had enjoyed so many precious years with John. She stayed with her sister-in-law for several days. Gladys later moved back to Denmark.

Beautiful carpets made by John and Gladys add colour to the floors in Hazel's home, and several of John's intricate counted cross-stitch pictures hang on the walls. Curios John brought back from his navy travels grace her cabinets. Several years later Hazel wrote, "The Lord took home my younger brother John in 1992 and my older brother Irvine in 1997. So now only Violet and I are left. We both are mobile and rejoicing in the Lord. We visit often by telephone and I visit her in Melfort, Saskatchewan, at least once a year."

Hazel still lives in her little house at 3425 Bethune Avenue. For several years she taught the Chronological Bible Course in Victoria, to the International Growth Group (mostly Filipino) and to the young people of the Vietnamese Church. She is active in Central Baptist Church and the Auxiliary of The Leprosy Mission Canada. Many OMF missionaries have retired in the Victoria area. Hazel seldom misses the monthly prayer meetings for OMF, The Leprosy Mission, Shantymen's Mission and Wycliffe Bible Translators, and the weekly prayer meeting at her church. She is friend and mentor to Filipino, Vietnamese, and Chinese people in Victoria.

She never did learn to drive in the city, so she walks to get groceries or mail letters, and hops on the bus to go downtown. Victoria is a city built on hills, so walking is all the exercise she needs. She is in good health, after receiving a pacemaker in 2001. The pacemaker gave her problems until she returned to the hospital so they could speed it up. She has had cataracts removed and still eats a well-balanced diet.

Beautiful flowering shrubs, flowers, grapevines, apples, pears, strawberries, raspberries, and plums fill her yard. She sells flowers to the local flower shops and blesses people continually with fresh fruit for jam.

Hazel was faithful to the Lord's call on her life, and Hazel's two terms of ministry in China stand like bookends, embracing the thirty-three years she spent in translation work in the Philippines. When asked how many languages she speaks, Hazel will humbly reply, "One at a time." However, the last count was twenty and it doesn't take her long to switch to another language when she hears someone speaking in their native tongue. The Lord has put her in a place where the cultures of the world come to her doorstep.

The Iraya New Testament has a place of honour on her coffee table. The Iraya/Tagalog/English dictionary is handy in a nearby bookcase. But perhaps what typifies Hazel's life most effectively is a medal, not even on display, but lovingly kept in a green velvet box. Presented by the Foreign Affairs Office, Shanghai Municipality, for special contributions to Shanghai, it is called the Magnolia Award. Only 124 foreigners, worldwide, had received this honour when it was awarded to Hazel. It is evidence of how Hazel,

215

God's Mimic, has and still does touch the lives of those around her. Her greatest rewards, though, come in the form of letters from her spiritual children all over the world. As they continue to spread the Gospel, her spiritual family continues to grow!

The Magnolia Award

# HAZEL'S CO-WORKERS

## MEXICO

Joyce Jenkins
Hazel Spotts
Lydia Zinke
Elizabeth (Sunny Beth) Soney

## CHINA

Edith Broadfoot
Doris Leonard
Hazel Waller
Anna Pfautz
Leita and Victor Christianson

## PHILIPPINES

Frances Williamson
Caroline Stickley
Morven Brown
Shirley Charlton
Elly van der Linden
Ann Flory
Daphne Parker
Hermann and Doris Elsaesser
Arlette Dombre

Printed in the United States
By Bookmasters